Motorbooks International

FARM TRACTOR COLOR HISTORY

OLIVER TRACTORS

Text by Robert N. Pripps
Photography by Andrew Morland

First published in 1994 by Motorbooks International Publishers & Wholesalers, PO Box 2, 729 Prospect Avenue, Osceola, WI 54020 USA

The information in this book is true and complete to the best of our knowledge. All recommendations are made without any guarantee on the part of the author or Publisher, who also disclaim any liability incurred in connection with the use of this data or specific details

We recognize that some words, model names and designations, for example,

mentioned herein are the property of the trademark holder. We use them for identification purposes only. This is not an official publication

Motorbooks International books are also available at discounts in bulk quantity for industrial or sales-promotional use. For details write to Special Sales Manager at the Publisher's address

Library of Congress Cataloging-in-Publication Data Available

Pripps, Robert N.
    Oliver tractors : Hart-Parr & Cockshutt / Robert N. Pripps, Andrew Morland.
        p.   cm. — (Motorbooks International farm tractor color history)
    Includes index.
    ISBN 0-87938-853-6
    1. Oliver tractors—History.
I. Morland, Andrew.   II. Title.
III. Series
TL233.5.P765   1994
629.225—dc20   93-39574

Printed and bound in Hong Kong

On the front cover: The Oliver Super 99 owned by Charlie Lulich of Mason, Wisconsin.

On the back cover: The 1947 Oliver 70 Row Crop wide-front owned by Everett Jensen of Clarks Grove, Minnesota, and the 1956 Cockshutt 35 Deluxe owned by Jim Grant of Georgetown, Ontario.

On the frontispiece: This 1938 Oliver 70 Standard is serial number 302959. Everett Jensen bought it from a dealer in Guide Rock, Nebraska. Everett bought his first Oliver in 1987. It was just like one his Dad had on the family farm. Jensen now has fifteen or sixteen restored Olivers, plus many other unrestored and non-Oliver machines. He is the Owner of Jensen's Outdoor Equipment in Clarks Grove, Minnesota, a lawn, garden, snowmobile sales and service establishment.

On the title pages: Lelah (left) and Cody, Carol Preuhs' registered quarterhorses seem unperturbed by the mechanical "horse" in their pasture. The tractor is a 1930 Oliver Hart-Parr Model A. The farm, owned by David and Carol Preuhs, near Le Center, Minnesota, has been in David's family since 1881. Besides being a farmer and tractor collector, David also has the interesting job of snow plowman for his local area. Several big (also antique) FWD trucks and a gigantic six-wheel-drive grader grace the property.

Contents

Preface

Firmly rooted in the early part of the Nineteenth Century, AGCO's White Tractor Division has one of the richest heritages in American agriculture. This book looks at two of its branches, Oliver and Cockshutt.

In doing the research for this book, I have gained a new appreciation of the complexities of fledgling companies such as these two. This is the story of entrepreneurs, of dreams, of risks, of bad economic times and good. If starting a success-ful business is hard today, it was virtually impossible in 1900. Finance, transportation, and communication were almost nonexistent; technical disciplines, such as engineering and metallurgy, were in their infancy.

This is also the story of tractor collectors. Those who love these old machines really love them! There are no more loyal and devoted fans than those of Oliver and Cockshutt. These following pages picture just a few of their prizes. These are the pictures Andrew Morland and I got during two weeks in June of 1992, plus those Andrew got while in Canada for a couple of days, earlier. Weather and scheduling problems prevented us from getting to as many collectors as we would have liked before Andrew had to return to England. We hope that the pictures of the beautiful antique tractors we did get will inspire more collectors and restorers to find and preserve such historic machinery.

Robert N. Pripps

Acknowledgments

I would like to gratefully acknowledge the contributions of several helpful people and organizations: Art Hammerstrom, director of marketing, AGCO, Norcross, Georgia; and R. J. Daniels, Belvidere, Illinois, my local White farm equipment dealer.

The Floyd County Historical Society and Museum, Charles City, Iowa, especially Mary Ann Townsend. This is the repository of all the Oliver Hart-Parr archives. A Hart-Parr No. 3 and the Oliver Experimental Tractor XO-121 are housed in this museum.

Many Oliver tractor collectors generously gave of their time and energies to provide information and photo opportunities for this book. Despite our best efforts, weather and scheduling difficulties prevented us from photographing some of their tractors, and we did not have space to include all the pictures we did take. We heartily apologize for these omissions. The pictures included here speak for themselves as to the loving dedication of the owners to their hobby.

Andrew Morland and I, as well as the staff and management of Motorbooks International, wish to extend our thanks to the following collectors: Rich Ramminger, Morrisonville, WI; Lynn Pollesch, Ripon, WI; Darrell Pollesch, Fox Lake, WI; Charlie Lulich of Lulich Implement, Mason, WI; Willis Pasche, Altura, MN; Walter Kellor, Kaukauna, WI; David Preuhs, Le Center, MN; Everett Jensen, Clarks Grove, MN; Earl Delp, Mt. Caroll, IL; and Jean L. Olson, Chatsfield, MN.

Oliver 66 Row Crop
A scaled down version of the 77, the Oliver 66 Row Crop was a seriously competitive tractor. It featured the six-speed transmission (with two reverse gears) and the same engine, except with four instead of six cylinders, as the 77. Originally available in gasoline and kerosene versions, in 1949 the kerosene engine was replaced by a diesel. Shown is the 66 Row Crop owned by the Pollesch Brothers.

Chapter 1

A Rich Heritage

Let us not forget that the cultivation of
the earth is the most important labor of man.
—*Daniel Webster*

We know from the Bible (Genesis 3:23) that Adam was a farmer, and we know that his first two sons, Cain and Able, were farmers. In fact, from the beginning until the 1750s, almost everyone was a farmer. If the above words of Daniel Webster were true of the Eighteenth Century, they were even more appropriate before, because so many were involved. Scholars of agricultural history, however, wonder why early man was not able to use his creativity to improve his tools for such a long time.

This does not mean that advancements were not made in agricultural methods and tools, but only that progress during these centuries was so painfully slow! The iron plow, for example, first appeared in the Near East around 1000 BC, but it was millenniums before it was widely used in the rest of the world. The earliest writings indicate that man saw the use of animals, mainly oxen

Oliver Hart-Parr advertisement
Oliver advertisement for the Oliver Hart-Parr Model A 18–36.

and donkeys, as labor savers in tillage and harvest. But each animal, itself, consumed the produce of about two acres. It was not until the last half of the Eighteenth Century that man began to raise himself above the curse of hard labor in wresting a living from the earth, or so it seemed.

Between 1750 and 1950, the number of people involved in agriculture dropped 80–90 percent. Most of that reduction occurred in the last quarter of those years, and most was in the developed regions of Europe and North America. In 1830, J.A. Blanqui, a French political economist, was struck by the rapidness of the changes in manufacturing, technology, and agriculture after 1750, calling it an "Industrial Revolution."

What factors fostered this so-called revolution and why did it wait until 1750 to begin? Many historians attribute its beginning to the combined usage of science and capital. Both had been available before, but they had not been applied together. The previous decades had seen the development of huge fortunes in shipping, mining, cottage industry, and feudal agriculture. As

the wealthy sought investment opportunities, scientific inventors came forward with ideas. Interrelated inventions fueled the revolution. George Stephenson in England and Robert Fulton in America showed the world how to use the power of steam for transportation. Samuel Morse invented the telegraph; Eli Whitney, the cotton gin; Elias Howe, the sewing machine; Sir Henry Bessemer, the steel-making process; Cyrus McCormick, the reaper; and John Pope, the threshing machine. None of these inventions by itself would have amounted to much, but together, they synergistically facilitated one another. The labor freed by the new machinery was used to staff the machinery factories. Industry was transferred from the home workshop to these factories. Machinery replaced manual labor to some degree in every area of life. Skilled specialists managed the great new enterprises, and marketing became global, rather than local and regional. The early 1800s were a time of great change, especially in agriculture, as farmers invented machines and the machines produced great industries.

Hart-Parr 30 "A"
Hart-Parr advertising copy stated that rim-type gear drive of the rear wheels relieved the spokes of drive stresses. To protect the gears from wear due to entrapment of dirt in the meshes, the oil from the Madison-Kipp oilers ran out on these meshes after it passed through the engine. Thus, this Hart-Parr 30 "A" had no crankcase oil sump. Oil must have been fairy cheap in those days, as consumption averaged about a half gallon per hour.

Mechanized Farming

Things happened rapidly in the late 1800s. James Oliver settled in Mishawaka, Indiana, in 1836, and began learning the foundry trade. A year later, another pioneer, John Deere, opened his plow-making business in Grand Detour, Illinois.

The Frost and Wood Company, a forerunner of the Cockshutt Plow Company of Ontario, Canada, was founded in 1839. Daniel Massey opened his farm equipment shop in Ontario, Canada, in 1840. In 1843, J. I. Case sold his first threshing machine and established his company in the Racine, Wisconsin, area. And in 1847, C. H. McCormick moved his reaper company to the recently incorporated frontier town of Chicago. The Industrial Revolution had come to American agriculture.

One can only imagine the tribulation the new "labor-saving" devices caused their new owners. Mechanical engineering was usually done by the trial-and-error method, and most farmers knew nothing about the workings of mechanical things. Much of American farmland at that

time was not that level, nor free of rocks and stumps, for machines such as McCormick's reaper to be fully used. Metal used for gears and shafts was brittle and did not wear well. And the early wooden threshers would often catch fire from overheated bearings. The early cast-iron plows were little better than the old wooden ones, because the heavy soils in much of the country stuck to the share and stopped the horses.

This was a time of intense and deleterious competition among the new farm equipment manufacturers. McCormick and Obed Hussey battled on the field and in court over the reaper market for more than thirty years. It all began in 1830, when McCormick's attention was diverted and he failed to patent the reaper he invented. Hussey had come up with

Cockshutt and Oliver 70 Standards
Cockshutt and Oliver 70 Standards stand side by side at the 1992 Stephenson County Antique Engine Club Show in Freeport, Illinois. Oliver and Cockshutt were the featured tractors in 1992, and some of the nicest restorations in the country were there. *Robert N. Pripps*

his own design, which he patented and began to market with alacrity. McCormick belatedly secured a patent on his own design and began serious production.

The War of the Reapers

By 1840, McCormick was beginning to enter the market in earnest. Due to some unfortunate changes, the popularity of the Hussey machine was beginning to wane. Hussey, feeling the pressure of competition, challenged McCormick to a field trial. By 1843, Hussey and Mc-

Cormick agreed to a public contest, to be held in the James River area of Virginia. Each machine was to harvest similar plots of the same field. The first one done was the winner. In two events, McCormick's reaper finished ahead of Hussey's, partly because of mechanical problems with the Hussey machine and partly due to the more difficult binding configuration, wherein the binders had to keep up with the machine. The Hussey reaper dropped the harvested grain in the path of the horse and machine when it made its next

round; the McCormick machine deposited the grain to the side, out of the way.

Hussey continued to challenge McCormick until his death in 1860

Previous page
Oliver 70 Row Crop
Everett Jensen is only the second owner of this 1947 Oliver 70 Row Crop. It is serial number 258910B, with the "B" indicating the rare wide-front configuration.

in a railroad accident. At just about the time that mechanical reaping was gaining wide acceptance with the farmers, the Hussey and Mc-Cormick patents ran out. Then there were many challengers on the market, all eager to take on the leaders in field trials. Mechanical reaping really caught on when the self-raker appeared on the market.

The Harvester War
Next came the self-tying binders, or harvesters, which made all of the old reapers obsolete. To quote author Merrill Denison from his book *Harvest Triumphant*: "Next to the wheel, the cutter bar, and the reel, the invention that did most for agricultural mechanization was the automatic knotter, the mechanism which did away with hand labor for the tying of the sheaves. It was this amazing device that transformed the reaper into the self-binder, a machine which has exerted a more profound influence on the world's economy than any other of man's technical accomplishments, save possibly the locomotive."

Hart-Parr 1913 Model
A 1913 Model Hart-Parr, of the type on display at the Floyd County Historical Society's museum in Charles City, Iowa.

Denison goes on to say that the self-binder saved 25 percent in harvesting manpower, and caused a real change in the rural-urban population split in the space of two decades.

Severe competition continued throughout the rest of the Nineteenth Century, as each of the major concerns tried to be first to acquire the manufacturing rights to promising new inventions. Each also fielded an army of sales agents who scrapped over every sale, sometimes

Hart-Parr advertisement
Hart-Parr magazine advertisement from 1912.

coming to blows. When a competitor learned of a pending sale, or even one that was essentially closed, he would pull his harvester and horses onto the farm and challenge the first manufacturer to a winner-take-all contest. Agents from other companies would hear of the competition and join in, and then the farmer's neighbors would come from miles around to watch. A carnival atmosphere ensued, with as many as fifty farmers attending and five manufacturers competing.

The intensity of this competition caused prices to drop to the point where profit margins were slim, at best. Advertising and promotional budgets soared, and when a sale was made, the salesman feted the customer lavishly. Often, the farmer's entire family would be invited to town to take delivery of the machine. A grand restaurant meal was usually provided. On one occasion, a McCormick agent had several machines to deliver on a certain day. He hired three bands and had floats made for a parade, with the customers riding in fancy carriages.

This, then, was the scene at the turn of the century. The drastic competition was good only for the farmer. He not only got much of his grain harvested during these wild field trials, but he also got the chance to buy machinery at rock-bottom prices. The manufacturers, however, soon got tired of this battle of wits, brawn, and technology. Amalgamations ensued until "trust busting" became fashionable in governmental circles. In 1891, Hart Massey and John Harris joined forces in Canada. McCormick and Deering, and three other smaller companies, joined to form International Harvester in 1902. Case and Deere, while remaining separate, did everything they could to acquire other companies to complete their product lines and to protect themselves from competition. Many smaller, specialty companies also merged for their own protection.

From Horse Power to Horsepower

During the first twenty years of the Twentieth Century, the full-line farm equipment manufacturers settled down to a gentlemanly level of competition, and added tractors to their lineups. To International Harvester, the biggest challenge was from the various state governments and the federal government, who kept the company in turmoil with "restraint of trade" charges as a result of the merger.

Case had been in the steam traction engine business since 1885, but in 1913 added internal combustion types to the line. International Harvester introduced tractors in 1906. Massey-Harris and John Deere bought existing tractors to add to their lists of farm implements in 1917 and 1918, respectively.

A phenomenon of this time, however, was the independent tractor maker. These included The Waterloo Gasoline Traction Engine Company, C. H. Dissinger and Bros. Company, and the Charter Gas Engine Company, all of which made tractors before 1900, but no other equipment. Another independent, Hart-Parr, the forerunner of Oliver, built its first tractor in 1902. It was the first designed for heavy drawbar work as well as for belt power. These gasoline traction engines, as they were then known, as well as those of the full-line manufacturers, were based on stationary engines. These engines, sometimes called farm powerplants, had proliferated mightily during the last twenty years of the Nineteenth Century.

The farm powerplant, indeed all engine development, had to wait for the petroleum industry to come up with a suitable fuel. Since man's beginnings, oil had been seeping to the surface of the earth. The Old Testament tells how the mother of Moses coated his cradle with pitch so that it would float on the Nile River. The Chinese were known to have used natural gas for fuel as far back as 1000 BC. Much surface oil was available in North America, and was used for lubrication, lighting, and medicine. In 1852, Canadian Abraham Gesner discovered the distilling

Hart Parr artwork
Cover of the Hart-Parr book, *Hart-Parr: Founders of the Tractor Industry.*

process for producing kerosene. Gasoline was a by-product that also had some use in lighting, but was generally discarded before the invention of the internal combustion engine.

Most successful and useful inventions claim many fathers. Such is the case with the internal combustion engine. The origin of the concept can be traced to the late-Seventeenth Century, when gunpowder "engines" were tried. The gunpowder was set off in a closed cylinder and the resultant pressure used to pump water. Turpentine, coal gas,

and natural gas engines were in use by 1800. In 1801, Lebon D'Humbersin, a Frenchman, patented an internal combustion engine in which the air and fuel vapors were mixed and pressurized in separate cylinders. An engine made by Stuart Perry of New York was patterned after a double-acting steam engine, with combustion occurring on both

15

ends of the piston at each end of the stroke. Perry's engine ran in 1844.

The internal combustion engine did not come to fruition, however, until the works of the great pioneers—Beau de Rochas, Lenoir, Brayton, Langen, and Nicholas Otto—were synergistically applied.

The internal combustion engine as a practical powerplant came into being in about 1880. That is when Nicholas Otto developed the Otto-cycle, or four-cycle, unit. Thermal efficiencies (the work obtained from the heat value of the fuel) now exceeded 12 percent. Such engines have been the mainstay of power production ever since.

By 1900, there were already 8,000 gasoline-powered automobiles in the United States. With the developments associated with automobiles—clutches, carburetors, ignition systems, drive trains, and steering mechanism—it is little wonder that gasoline engines were soon mounted on running gear, first to make the engine portable and later to have it pull like the horse.

These first twenty years of the Twentieth Century saw gasoline (and kerosene) traction engines grow to monstrous proportions in competition with the steam engine. Hart-Parr's 1907 60hp model weighed more than ten tons. Little effort was made to compete with the horse until about 1914, when such smaller tractors as the Bull, the Moline Universal, and the Allis-Chalmers three-wheel came on the scene. Henry Ford, of Model T Ford fame, also began with "press releases" about a low-cost, mass-produced Model T-like tractor at that time. His Fordson

Oliver Hart-Parr 70 Row Crop
The Oliver Hart-Parr 70 Row Crop took the tractor industry by storm when introduced in 1935. It was one of the finest examples of competitive overkill seen up to that time, rivaled perhaps, only by Ford's V-8 engine. This 1936 model is owned by Everett Jensen of Clarks Grove, Minnesota.

tractor hit the agricultural world like a torpedo in late 1917, just as the first World War reached its peak.

World War I changed the world more than most people today fully appreciate, especially concerning agriculture. When the war started, Canada, Russia, and the United States were the leading wheat producers. During the previous fifty years before World War I, both immigrants and several varieties of wheat, capable of surviving the dry, windy conditions and fine, dusty soil of the North American Great Plains, were imported from the Steppes of Russia. The wheats were the "Turkey Red" and "Red Fife" varieties, with hard kernels and short stems. The immigrants were Mennonites, fleeing religious persecution and military service. They settled on lands of the Great Plains given them by the railroad companies, and proceeded to show the other homesteaders how to grow wheat.

In 1914, the Turkish Navy blockaded the Dardanelles, effectively shutting off the flow of Russian wheat to the rest of the world. Suddenly, it was up to the farmers of the great American plains to make up for the loss. Simultaneously, much of Europe's food growing was disrupted by the war. American farmers began plowing up all the acreage they could get, sparking more demand for tractors. By 1920, there were twice as many plowed acres in the Great Plains as in 1910. At the same time, the price of wheat more than doubled. The resultant prosperity for the farmers allowed them to buy more land and machinery. Wheat farming became so profitable that absentee speculators would buy great pieces of land; they would buy equipment, till it, and plant wheat in the fall. The following summer, they would return to harvest the crop.

With impeccable timing, the Fordson burst on the scene on October 8, 1917. Although fewer than 300 were

Fordson
A 1920 version of the Fordson tractor. By 1920, Ford owned almost three-quarters of the world's tractor market. This meteoric rise in popularity dramatically changed the concept of the tractor from that of a steam-engine competitor to that of a horse competitor.

made that year, the concept of the light, small, mass-produced, and inexpensive tractor was realized. The timing was right, because the turmoil then boiling up in Europe was soon also to involve America. The Lloyd-George government in Great Britain was desperate to get American food production equipment before US industry was tied up with war production. The British Board

of Agriculture sought both tractor imports and production rights to American tractors. In this regard, Henry Ford was approached about the possibility of sending some of his soon-to-be mass-produced Fordsons to England. Even though Ford was a pacifist, he generously made a gift of the patent rights to the Fordson to the British Board of Agriculture. He also agreed to set up a factory to produce them in Cork, Ireland; and, in 1918, shipped 7,000 to Britain.

The Tractor War

For the next two years, Ford garnered more than 75 percent of the world tractor market, selling about 75,000 units per year. Business was

not bad for the other tractor producers either. Despite the competition of the Fordson, the demand for farm produce and rising prices caused an even greater demand for tractors. By 1921, however, a post-war depression caused a severe downturn in sales. Henry Ford's tractor "engine" was running, though, and a way had to be found for him to move more tractors. Thus began the tractor price war of the Twenties. Ford cut his prices throughout the year from $700 to $625, and finally made a dramatic cut to $395. Ford was testing the elasticity of demand.

C. H. McCormick III, in his book, *The Century of the Reaper*, wrote, "The harvester war of the 1890s was cruel, disastrous to the weaker combatants, and yet it was inspiring in the way its testing brought out the finer qualities of men. But in the first twenty International years, competition had perhaps become routine. Henry Ford's presence in the implement province and the new type of competition he soon introduced returned the industry for a time to the atmosphere of battle." In any case, Fordsons sold; other brands did not. The year 1922 saw Fordson production back to around the 70,000 unit level, and in 1923, it was more than 100,000.

International Harvester countered with the 10–20 McCormick Deering in 1922. Others, such as Case and John Deere, brought out new, smaller, lighter, less expensive models as well. Nevertheless, Ford still carried more than 60 percent of the market. Competition from the Fordson eliminated many companies from the field over the next several years, including the mighty General Motors entry, the Samson.

By 1929, when the Oliver Hart-Parr merger was consummated, the great tractor war was over. Of the 166 listed for 1920, only forty-seven tractor manufacturers were left; they were still producing just a few over 100,000 units per year. By then, both the Fordson and the Model T were also gone from the scene. Henry Ford said he stopped production of the Fordson because he needed the space for construction of the new Model A car. The Model A was birthed in 1928 to replace the Model T. The facts are that the Fordson, as well as the Model T, were overtaken by determined competition. In the case of the Model T, it was the Chevrolet automobile. In the case of the Fordson, it was the Farmall tractor. The Farmall, introduced by International Harvester in 1924, unveiled a totally new era in the tractor business. No longer was the steam engine the competition. Now the tractor had taken on the horse. From now on, the tractor would be required to do more than just pull

FARMALL Plowing and Belt Work Simply Can't Be Surpassed!

THERE is enthusiasm for the work of the FARMALL wherever this perfected tractor appears. On all crops, on all jobs in field and barnyard, it shows the power farmer *something new in handling and efficiency*.

Plowing is one of its strongest suits. The FARMALL owner goes out to tackle that once-dreaded job with interest and good humor. He has learned that FARMALL and its plow will move handily and rapidly over the fields and leave well-turned furrows behind, in ideal shape for the operations and the crops to follow.

On belt work it is the same. We have dozens of positive letters from owners.

D. M. Hastings of Atlanta, Ga., writes, "You deserve a pat on the back for the FARMALL. Please do not thank me for this as it is well deserved." He has used his FARMALL on every kind of work including many belt jobs.

Remember that the Harvester engineers devoted several years to working out this *all-purpose, all-crop, all-year design*. They tried out thoroughly *every* type of design. When FARMALL was *right for all drawbar, belt and power take-off work* they offered it to the farmer. The FARMALL is *the one all-purpose tractor that plants and cultivates, too*. It is the feature of power farming today.

Begin by asking the McCormick-Deering dealer where you can see a FARMALL on the job

INTERNATIONAL HARVESTER COMPANY
of America (Incorporated)
606 So. Michigan Ave.   Chicago, Illinois

... And next spring your FARMALL will be all ready to go at the PLANTING and CULTIVATING jobs. It's that kind of a tractor!

with the draw bar or power with its belt pulley. Now tractors would be required to power implements, such as binders and mowers, with power take-off (PTO) shafts; and they would be required to mount integral cultivators and plows, which could be lifted through engine power. The age of the "all-purpose" tractor had arrived.

Farmall advertisement
A 1927 advertisement for the radical new Farmall from International Harvester.

Chapter 2

The Birth of the Tractor Industry

The origin of the word "tractor" is credited to
the year 1906 and to W. H. Williams, sales manager
of the Hart-Parr Company.
—*R.B. Gray*

It may come as a surprise to some that the very first steam powerplant was invented by a scientist named Hero, who lived in Egypt 120 years before the birth of Christ. Hero's engine consisted of a hollow globe mounted on a pipe running to a steam kettle. Two L-shaped pipes were fastened to opposite sides of the globe. With a fire burning under the kettle, steam rushed out of the L-shaped pipes, the reaction forces causing the globe to rotate in the opposite direction.

More than 1,600 years passed before steam power would be harnessed. These first "engines" operated on the principle that when steam condensed back into water in a closed container, a vacuum was created. This vacuum was used to lift water, raising it out of mines. James Watt invented several of the features that made the steam engine a practical powerplant, including the separate condenser, the crankshaft, the double-acting expansion engine, the throttle valve, and governor.

Around the turn of the Eighteenth Century, steam power was applied to transportation. A Frenchman named Nicolas Cugnot is said to have made the first self-propelled vehicle in 1769, but it wasn't until 1800 that Richard Trevithick in England and Oliver Evans in America began running steam land machines; and Robert Fulton made the first successful steamboat, the *Clermont*, in 1808.

Farm steam power, stoked by the inventions of the reaper and thresher, came first on the scene in 1841 in the form of an engine by Ransomes of England. Next came "The Forty-Niner," built in 1849 by A. L. Archambault of Philadelphia. Garr-Scott followed these in 1852, then Robinson in 1860, Rumely in 1862, and J. I. Case in 1869. The early ones were steam power units only, with no self-moving capabilities. The self-propelling feature and the ability to pull loads began to appear in the late 1850s. One of the first more-or-less successful of these was the Fawkes Steam Plow, made in 1858. Others followed in short order, but all were big and heavy and expensive, and suitable for only the largest farms. By 1880, the steam traction engine was a mature device which found routine use in plowing, land clearing, and belt-powering a variety

of farm implements. By the start of the Twentieth Century, thirty-one steam engine manufacturers were producing around 5,000 engines per year.

Adding the traction feature to the portable steam farm engine was a larger step than is commonly appreciated. First was the problem of routinely moving the steamer with steam pressure up. A system of springs had to be incorporated to isolate the boiler from road shocks. Next, the drive train, clutch, differential, and reversing mechanism had to be invented. Finally, a system of operator controls had to be perfected, which included steering. Over the forty-or-so years that the steam traction engine ruled, the con-

Hart-Parr 30 "A"
The Hart-Parr 30 "A" was a two-cylinder, four-cycle machine. The engine bore and stroke were 6.50x7.00in. Operating speed was 750rpm. It had a two speed transmission providing forward speeds of 1.98mph and 2.88mph. The 30 was the subject of the 26th Nebraska Tractor Test, where it demonstrated a maximum drawbar pull of nearly 3,500lb.

figurations of those produced by the various manufacturers became quite similar. Therefore, it is little wonder that early internal combustion tractors were very similar in construction.

The Otto-Cycle Engine

The first internal combustion engines, like the first steam engines, pumped water with the vacuum created in the cylinder as the heat dissipated. Abbe' Hautefeuille of France invented such an engine in 1678, using gunpowder to create the heat.

With the advent of the practical steam engine, it was only a matter of time until the arrival of the internal combustion engine. Before internal combustion was practical, however, a suitable fuel (gasoline) and suitable metals had to be found.

In the earliest internal combustion engines, an "explosive" mixture was set off above the piston, which was at the top of its stroke. There was no attempt to first compress the mixture. As in the steam engine, compression was done in the boiler and the cylinder was merely an expander, with the heat raising the pressure to move the piston within the cylinder.

The cycle on which an internal combustion engine operates distinguishes one type from another. The cycle is defined as the series of changes through which each charge passes on its way through the engine. The changes include those of volume, pressure, or chemical action. Beau de Rochas first came up with the idea of compressing the combustible mixture before ignition, but it was up to Nicholas Otto in 1876 to develop an engine that had compression, expansion, exhaust, and intake cycles: the four-cycle, or Otto-cycle engine.

Two factors delayed the acceptance of the four-cycle engine. Most early experimenters could not accept the perceived disadvantage of only one power stroke for every two revolutions. Furthermore, Otto had

the concept fairly well tied up with patents. By 1890, these two factors were largely being ignored, and the four-cycle engine rapidly gained universal acceptance.

Early gas engines, as these internal combustion powerplants were called in those days, were generally one- or two-cylinder affairs. Progress in carburetion occurred rapidly, but ignition systems were problematical. Initially tried was a pilot light-type of ignition, through which the pre-pressurized fuel-air mixture was passed on its way into the combustion chamber. Heated ceramic "glow-plugs" were used next, followed by "low-tension," or low-voltage, spark switches in the combustion chamber. Finally, the high-tension system, with its attendant magneto and spark plugs, made its way onto the scene.

Cooling of the early gas engine was also a point of some controversy among the approximately 100 builders at the turn of the century. Since cast-iron had a melting point of 2300deg F and combustion temperatures were approaching 3000deg, the engine had to be cooled. Most of the smaller, cheaper engines merely added a tank of water around the cylinder assembly. Relying on the latent heat of vaporization, the liquid water kept the cylinder at a constant water-boiling temperature, although the water level slowly diminished as steam was lost.

A 1909 college textbook entitled *The Gas Engine*, by Forest R. Jones, explained the process: "When a charge is burned in a motor, part of the heat is abstracted by the enclosing walls, part is transformed into mechanical energy, and the remainder passes out with the exhaust gases. The only useful part, as far as the motor is concerned, is that transformed into mechanical energy. The cooler the confining walls, the greater the amount of heat abstracted from the gasses by them. The transformation of the heat of the fuel into

mechanical energy is therefore more efficient the hotter the walls."

Thus, with water cooling limited to the boiling temperature of water, designers turned to a liquid with a higher boiling temperature: oil. In addition to a boiling temperature of 300degF, oil cooling had two other advantages: It had a low freezing temperature, and leaks into the crankcase were not deleterious. The oil was not allowed to boil, but was circulated through a radiator. With oil, more heat could be rejected by a radiator than with water.

Following the course set by the steam engine, the early farm gas engine was mounted first on skids to make it portable, and then on wagon running gear. Traction engine development generally consisted of mounting a suitable gas engine on a steam engine chassis. The first recorded production (six were built) tractor was the 1889 Charter. A 15hp gas Charter engine was mounted on a Rumely steam engine chassis.

In 1892, John Froelich mounted a Van Duzen engine on a Robinson steam running gear. The machine had an operator's platform in front and a steering wheel, and could propel itself backward and forward. The 20hp engine operated on gasoline. During the 1892 harvest season, Froelich used the machine in a custom threshing operation lasting fifty days. He both pulled and powered a Case 40x58 thresher, harvesting 72,000 bushels of small grain. A year later, Froelich was instrumental in forming the Waterloo Gasoline Traction Engine Company of Waterloo, Iowa. This company eventually produced the Waterloo Boy tractor, the forerunner of the John Deere tractor line.

The company's early efforts did not, however, pay off in the first commercially viable tractor. That honor goes to two men named Charles, of Charles City, Iowa: Charles Hart and Charles Parr.

In 1891, the year before the Froelich, the William Deering Com-

Hart-Parr
A 1904 Hart-Parr, photographed at the 1992 Pontiac, Illinois, thresheree. *Robert N. Pripps*

pany mounted its two-cylinder 6hp engine on a New Ideal mower, making it self-propelled. For the next several years, Deering, which had not yet merged with McCormick to form International Harvester, made several other self-propelled farm machines, but not tractors per se.

The McCormick Company also developed its own engines beginning in 1897, installing them the next year on its own running gears and marketing them as traction engines. After the formation of International Harvester in 1902, interest in and work on tractors accelerated. Harvester was among the first of the long-line implement companies to

offer a tractor, introducing its first model in 1906. This first unit typifies the problems of the time, as its single-cylinder engine was mounted on rollers so that it could be moved back and forth to engage a friction drive. The engine had an open crankcase and used spray-tank cooling. The same year that McCormick built its first engine, 1897, Hart and Parr began their farm engine business while still university students.

The Hart-Parr Tractor Company

These two men named "Charles" are credited with birthing the tractor industry in a place along the Cedar River in Iowa called Charles City.

Charles W. Hart and Charles H. Parr met while engineering students at the University of Wisconsin.

According to an article by E. M. Wooley in the January 1914 *The World's Work*, from an early age Hart had an Horatio Alger-like dream of power farming. His father, who had three farms near Charles City, thought going to college—and traction engines—were folly. Young Hart prevailed, however, and enrolled in

23

Charles W. Hart
Charles W. Hart, co-founder of the Hart-Parr Company, lived from 1872–1937. As a young man, he dreamed of the benefits of power farming. He eventually brought the company to his hometown of Charles City, Iowa.

Hart-Parr factory
The Hart-Parr plant in Charles City, Iowa, in full swing circa 1910.

Iowa State College of Agriculture and Mechanical Arts at Ames. At the age of twenty, Hart transferred to the University of Wisconsin, where he found the faculty more receptive to helping him pursue his goal. It was here that Charles Parr caught Hart's infectious enthusiasm for engines.

Together, and with the help of their instructors, they built three working engines, one of which is still on display at the university. Be-

Charles H. Parr
Charles H. Parr, co-founder of the Hart-Parr Company, lived from 1868–1941.

fore their graduation in 1897, they had formed the Hart-Parr Gasoline Engine Company, specializing in oil-cooled farm gas engines. Based upon their demonstrated engines, they were able to borrow $3,000 locally to set up the gas engine company, but investors were not interested in gasoline traction engines.

Towards the end of 1899, Charles Hart paid a visit to his folks in Charles City. He complained to his father that development funds could not be found for his tractor project.

"There's money around here that might be interested," replied the elder Hart, admitting for the first time that his son's ambition was not folly.

In 1900, as the engine business expanded, Hart and Parr decided to move their company from Madison to Charles City. At this point, a third

Hart-Parr factory
The birthplace of the tractor industry: an aerial view of the Charles City, Iowa, plant, taken in 1963.

Charles entered the scene: a Charles City lawyer and banker named Charles D. Ellis. Ellis was born in New York in 1850 and moved to Charles City with his family in 1867, after his father purchased a farm there. He studied law and in 1872, went into law practice in Charles City. Later, his older brother was also admitted to the bar and joined the firm, which was then called Ellis and Ellis.

He agreed to provide a $50,000 loan and to purchase stock in the company, now to be called the Hart-Parr Company. A new, larger factory was also made available. With financing and more factory space, work was begun on Hart's dream project: a gasoline traction engine.

Hart-Parr Number 1 was completed in 1902. It was powered by a two-cylinder, four-cycle horizontal engine with the crankshaft cross-wise to the direction of travel. The valve-in-head engine had a 9in bore and 13in stroke and produced 30 belt horsepower at 250rpm. The ignition was of the low-tension type; it used batteries for starting and a low-voltage generator during operation. The cooling medium was oil, but commercial household heating radiators were used to reject the heat to the atmosphere. The chassis was more or

Hart-Parr Number 1
Note the home-type radiator and expansion bulbs used for cooling the engine. Hart-Parr pioneered the use of oil as a cooling medium as it had a higher boiling temperature than water. High operating temperatures were desirable when using kerosene fuel. *The Smithsonian Institution*

less the same as the typical steam traction engine. The machine was designed for traction work, which allowed it to provide reliable service with as many as five 14in plows.

By the end of 1903, fifteen variations of this original theme were completed and sold. Later units had up to 45 belt horsepower, and most used oil radiators designed specifically for this purpose. These radiators were cooled by air flow induced by engine exhaust in a manner similar to the way draft was induced on the typical steamer.

Customers did not immediately beat the proverbial path, however. Hart-Parr was able to field only one salesman to run demonstrations at county fairs and other events. Competitors thoroughly roasted the gasoline upstart. But Hart was patient. "We can't force it," he said, "we have to let it simmer into the market." The competition became so vociferous that potential customers began to get suspicious about how much they were protesting.

Little by little, the Hart-Parrs began to garner defenders. Some of the first tractors delivered were gaining a reputation of usefulness that far surpassed that of the steamers, and in another two years, the tide began to turn.

"If it hadn't been for the free publicity given by our friends, the enemy," said Hart, "I really don't know if we should have pulled through."

In subsequent years, Hart-Parr produced a 17–30 model and an 18–30 model; pioneered the use of the less-expensive fuel, kerosene; and became the country's largest producer of tractors. By 1907, one-third of all tractors (about 600) in America were Hart-Parrs.

W. H. Williams, sales manager in 1906, decided the words "traction engine" were vague and too long to use in press releases, so he coined the word "tractor" instead. For this reason, and because the Charles City plant was the first to be continuously and exclusively used for tractor production, Hart-Parr has been given the title of "Founders of the Tractor Industry."

In 1907, Hart-Parr built a 60 belt horsepower behemoth model called "Old Reliable." These proved to be ideal for work on the larger farms of the Great Plains. Through the beginning of the Great Tractor War of the 1920s, more than 1,000 of these ten-ton monsters were sold.

As World War I was ending, and the Tractor War of the Twenties was getting under way, major changes began to happen at Hart-Parr. Some friction also began to develop between the two tractor pioneers and their business partner, the banker Ellis. With the impact of the Fordson not yet completely established, Ellis pushed for lighter, smaller, more Fordson-like tractors. Although the inventors resisted, the New Hart-Parr 18–25 emerged in late 1918. It had a water-cooled, two-cylinder, four-cycle engine that operated at 750rpm; a high-tension magneto ignition system; a fan-cooled radiator using a friction drive; and a two-speed transmission. Most importantly, this tractor looked like a tractor—that is, it looked much like what was rapidly becoming the conventional tractor, with a radiator in front, gas tank above the engine, and an uncovered operator platform on the back.

All these changes were too much for Hart and Parr to accept, and they

sold their stock to Ellis. They stayed with the company for a few more years, but both eventually left. Hart moved to Montana, where he took up farming (he was only forty-eight at the time), and Parr remained in Charles City until his death in 1941 at the age of seventy-three. Hart lived in Montana until he died at the age of sixty-five.

Charles Ellis continued operating the company, producing approximately ten more tractor models, plus stationary engines, road graders, and

washing machines. In 1928, failing health forced him to turn control of the Hart-Parr Company over to his son, Melvin W. Ellis. In 1929, M. W. Ellis merged Hart-Parr with three other companies: Nichols & Shepard Threshing Machine Company, American Seeding Machine Company, and Oliver Chilled Plow Works. The resultant company was known as the Oliver Farm Equipment Company. Charles Ellis died in 1933 at the age of eighty-three.

Hart-Parr artwork
"Hart-Parr Power" from the cover of an early Hart-Parr brochure.

Chapter 3

James Oliver, The Man and His Company

The sluggard will not plow by reason of the cold;
therefore shall he beg in the harvest, and have nothing.
—Proverbs 20:4
(From a wall plaque in James Oliver's office)

They say that the character of a corporation reflects the character of the person at the top. This was certainly true of the Oliver Chilled Plow Company, but it is also true, to a great extent, of the entities that spawned from it, even today.

Today, the giant AGCO conglomerate of Norcross, Georgia, which inherited the Oliver assets, by then folded into White Farm Equipment, is one of the most customer-oriented companies in the business. James Oliver's strength of character becomes even more apparent when one considers that he died in 1908, before his company even became involved in tractors. Yet his legacy of Scottish values of discipline, self-reliance, and hard work lives on.

Oliver Hart-Parr 70 Row Crop
Some of the features of the new Oliver Hart-Parr 70 Row Crop that bowled over the competition in 1935 were a six-cylinder engine with starter and generator, pleasing styling, and a colorful paint scheme. The engine was equipped with an oil-wash air cleaner and featured pressure lubrication. The tractor had a four-speed transmission and offered a powered implement lift.

James Oliver was born in Liddesdale, Roxburghshire, Scotland, on August 28, 1823. He was the youngest of eight children: six boys and two girls. His father was a shepherd. Times were hard as James came into the family (it is said that Scottish sheep developed sharp noses to get at the grass between the rocks), but the frugal family managed to get along. Opportunities for young people were so limited that, in 1830, oldest-brother John came to America. He found work near Geneva, New York, for a dollar a day. Soon he began sending home glowing letters describing a land where the forests were actually in the way and where people ate meat three times a week.

This was too much for Andrew and Jane, the next two oldest, and they followed in 1832. Three children gone to America exerted an emotional pull on their mother, and besides, all three were thriving there while those in Scotland were barely eking out an existence. James' father was not of the adventurist type, however, and resisted the idea of moving the rest of the family. Finally, Mrs. Oliver took charge and announced that the family was immigrating to America. The year was 1834; Jamie, as he was called, was eleven.

The family landed in Garden Castle, New York, after crossing the Atlantic in a sailing vessel. James later recounted that as a bewildered lad on the dock, he was given an orange by one man and a kick by another—he never forgot either.

The family proceeded to Albany by steamboat, to Schenectady by rail, and then to Geneva, where John, Andrew, and Jane lived and worked, by canal boat on the Erie Canal. For the first time in his young life, Jamie had plenty to eat: meat, potatoes, onions, and corn on the cob. (Young Jamie reportedly sent the cob back for a refill.) Jamie went to work for a farmer for fifty cents per week plus room and board. The pay wasn't much, even for an eleven-year-old boy; possibly the farmer had seen him eat. To add insult to injury, the farmer said he would have paid him more if he spoke English!

Two years later, a group of the New York Scottish families, the Olivers included, decided to move

James Oliver
James Oliver, circa 1900, developer of the Oliver Chilled Plow and founder of the Oliver tractor firm.

west to Indiana, because of new laws regarding homesteading the frontier lands. They first landed in La Grange County, but later moved to Mishawauka, in St. Joseph County, where Andrew had settled. Mishawauka thrived on the mining of bog iron, which was transported up the St. Joseph River to Lake Michigan. Here, James was afforded one year of schooling, but that abruptly ended when his father died in 1837.

James then hired himself out to the owner of a pole-boat plying the river with iron, for $6 per week. He took $5 of it home to his mother. Although James liked the river, he did not take to the rowdy life of a riverman. Boat polers were paid in part with whiskey, and lived accordingly. James said that he had a desire to be decent and to be with decent people.

In addition to his riverboat job, James did odd jobs around Mishawauka. On one occasion, James dug a ditch and split some shingles for a man named Joseph Doty. The Dotys, an old English family, lived in one of Mishawauka's nicer homes. As was the custom, James was given meals with the Doty family while he was working. It was then that he began using bear grease on his unruly red hair; those who noticed concluded it was because of Doty's daughter, Susan. Susan's disdain for rivermen soon came to Oliver's attention, so he quit that occupation and began to learn the iron molding trade.

Bad times in the iron business saw James also learn the cooper's trade. Here, the going rate of pay was one dollar per day. Young Oliver saw an opportunity for his Scottish work ethic to pay off and so prevailed upon his employer to pay him to make barrel staves on a piece-work basis. He was soon making two dollars a day.

Meanwhile, Oliver spent as much time with Susan Doty as possible. With her help, he read most of the fifty books in the Doty library. Love blossomed, much to the consternation of Englishman Doty. Although he objected to the match, Doty (unaware of Oliver's handsome income from the barrel factory) indicated that he would relent to the marriage if young Oliver could meet the seemingly impossible condition of owning a house. James soon located a family eager to leave Mishawauka for the frontier town of Ft. Dearborn (Chicago). They were willing to sell their two-room bungalow, with a pounded blue clay floor, for $20— and throw in the lot as well since, they reasoned, land in Indiana wasn't worth anything. James' offer of $18, cash, was accepted; so was James' offer to Susan. They were married in 1844.

James Oliver worked at molding, coopering, and farming until he was

thirty-two years old. By then, he and Susan had a $1,000 house and a quarter-section of land. They also had two children, Joseph D. and Josephine.

It was at this time that an event occurred in the life of James Oliver that would greatly affect his future, the future of many others, and the future of agriculture worldwide. While in South Bend on business, Oliver met a man who wanted to sell a quarter interest in his foundry at inventory value ($88.96). Oliver happened to have $100 in his pocket at the time. Thus, in 1855, James Oliver found himself in the cast-iron

business in the role of management, rather than that of a worker. One of the products of the foundry was a cast-iron plow, and James knew plows! None that he had tried were satisfactory.

"The man," said James Oliver, quoted in Elbert Hubbard's *James Oliver: Little Journeys*, "who has never been jerked up astride his plow handles, or been flung into the furrow by a balky plow has never had his vocabulary tested. A good plow should stay in the ground without wearing out the man at the handles. A plow should be light as is consistent with endurance and

Oliver Chilled Plow
An early example of the Oliver Chilled Plow. James Oliver considered development of the plow an artform and made variations on the theme for every type of soil condition. Note the fancy floral design on the beam. *The Smithsonian Institution*

good work; the moldboard should scour, so as to turn the soil with a singing sound."

The Oliver Chilled Plow
In today's no-till, or low-till, environment, we sometimes forget the

importance of the plow and plowing to the farmer, even just a few years ago. Before the age of chemicals, a farmer's two main jobs were plowing and cultivating.

The purpose of plowing is to pulverize the soil and to cover field trash. The tilled soil must have good contact with the subsoil to facilitate the rise of moisture. Air spaces, bunches of trash, and sod clods impede root growth and break the contact with the subsoil. The plow also covers and mixes in manure fertilizer.

Crude iron plows appeared in the Near East about 1000 BC, but it wasn't until the Eighteenth Century that the cast-iron plow was known in the western world. Charles Newbold obtained the first American patent for a cast-iron plow in 1797. With typical resistance to anything new, however, the American farmer feared that the iron plow would poison the soil and promote the growth of weeds. The superiority of iron over wood was quickly recognized and by 1819, a cast-iron plow maker named Jethro Woods was turning out 4,000 per year.

Ordinary cast-iron is by nature rough and full of surface imperfections known as blow-holes. It does not take a polish and is prone to rusting, which further pits the surface. The ordinary cast-iron plow worked well enough in the light, sandy soils of the eastern states, but as one went west, the soil got heavier. Brown silt loam was found on the plains of Indiana and a sticky black gumbo was in Illinois and farther west. In the north, there was also a full complement of gravel and rocks (winter potatoes). Cast-iron plow makers added as standard equipment a leather pouch containing a wooden paddle, not unlike a modern-day windshield ice scraper. In many cases, the plowman could travel only a few yards before he had to roll the plow on its side and scrape the "mud" from the moldboard.

Before 1864, when Bessemer steel was first made commercially in the United States, steel cost about 25¢ per pound. Thus, while it was available throughout the Nineteenth Century, it was used only where its superior strength or other properties were essential.

Steel is an alloy of iron and small, but definite, quantities of carbon and other materials. It is stronger than iron and can be formed in ways that iron cannot. The surface of steel is smooth and it takes a high polish. Wrought-iron, which is iron mixed with iron silicate, has many of the properties of steel, but on a lower order.

In 1837, when John Deere made his famous steel plow from a discarded sawmill blade, there were many plow makers and many plow patents across the United States and Canada. Because transportation was so limited, many of these sold only to a local area and production volumes were very low. Deere, for example, is said to have built just 225 plows in his first six years in the business. There were other plow makers using steel before John Deere, but the cost and availability caused most, including Deere, to use wrought- and cast-iron in as many places as possible. When James Oliver bought into the South Bend foundry, cast-iron was the material of choice for plows because of cost. The other materials were often added, as necessary, to the moldboard, share, and shin, but costs went up disproportionately. In heavy soil areas, farmers either bore the additional cost or used the scraping paddle.

James Oliver worked on producing a better cast-iron plow for twelve years before achieving success. The Bible verse, Isaiah 2:4, "and they shall beat their swords into plowshares...," stuck in his mind. He was further inspired by the "Toledo Blade," a shining sword with a keen edge, lightness, and tremendous strength. To make such a moldboard

was his ambition. The molder of the sword, in Toledo, Spain, was known to quench the white hot blade with water to give it its temper. The bulk of the cast-iron plow caused differential contraction when quenched, and it warped hopelessly.

The main features of Oliver's development were in ribbing and grooving the casting and in chilling the surface while allowing the core to cool more slowly. Oliver's process made the plow's face hard so that it wore well, but left the inner metal less tempered and brittle, and more resilient. The chilling process left the orientation of the fibers of the metal perpendicular to the surface. This gave wearing resistance and a surface smoothness that exceeded that of steel.

At the same time, Oliver began to have success with some other experiments in plow design. These mostly had to do with controlling the line of draft so that it was reflected upon the center of the moldboard. Oliver, Deere, Case, and others also began to use the rolling plow shape still characteristic of plows today. These features gave the Oliver Chilled Plow a draft load of about half that of the old cast-iron plow, and at a competitive cost. Within years, Oliver was selling seven times as many plows as his nearest competitor.

With all this success, James Oliver never ceased to be a farmer. He and his men went all over the United States studying plowing methods and problems and devising plow variations to meet the different conditions. Eventually, the Oliver plow catalog had more than 1,000 combinations. "I am a partner with the farmer, and the farmer is a partner with nature," he used to say. He always looked forward to the time when he could turn the company over to son Joseph and go back to farming full time.

Oliver had strong opinions about many things in business and farming, and was never reticent to express them. One of these was his positive view on the value of Clydesdales compared with Percherons. He so loved the Clydes that for many years he drove a shaggy-legged half-breed to his buggy. He declared that all a good Clyde needed to make him a race horse was patience and training. He said the horse he drove was really quite a fast trotter—"if I would let him out."

The Oliver Chilled Plow Company was heavily courted at the turn of the century when organizing manufacturing trusts became the rage. When Oliver was last approached on the theme, he replied, "I do not care for your money, neither do I nor my family wish to get out of business. We are not looking for ease or rest or luxury. I love this institution, and if I go into this combine, granting I make more money than now, what is to prevent your shutting down these works and throwing all these people who have worked for me all these years out of employment? And how would that affect this city, which has been my home and the home of those I love? No, sir, your talk of more money and less responsibility means nothing to me. I want my children to always feel the stress and strain of work, and never to forget the burdens of life, in order that they may respect the burdens of others."

James Oliver died in 1908 at the age of eighty-five. Joseph D. Oliver became head of the company. Joseph had rare gifts for organization and marketing, and the company continued to thrive and expand. It was Joseph who led the company into the amalgamation with Hart-Parr and others in 1929 to form the Oliver Farm Equipment Company.

Chapter 4

Oliver Hart-Parr Tractors

[The farm tractor] like every other major invention...
has increased the relative advantage of ability
and education and the possession of capital...
and imposes a corresponding handicap on those
who lack these qualities.
—*H.W. Peck, 1927*

On April 1, 1929, four companies merged to form the Oliver Farm Equipment Company, later known as the Oliver Corporation. These were Oliver Chilled Plow Works Company (1855), Hart-Parr Tractor Company (1897), Nichols & Shepard Threshing Machine Company (1848), and American Seeding Machine Company (1840). The backgrounds of the first two of these were covered previously. Because the involvement of the later two do not have a large impact on tractor heritage, they will only be covered briefly.

Nichols & Shepard Threshing Machine Company

John Nichols, a blacksmith, established his shop in Battle Creek, Michigan, in 1848. Like other blacksmiths of the time, he manufactured farm tools for the local trade. He built his first threshing machine in 1852. It was so successful, and business was so good, that he took on David Shepard as a partner.

In 1866, the two became the first to incorporate their business under the laws of Michigan, and the new

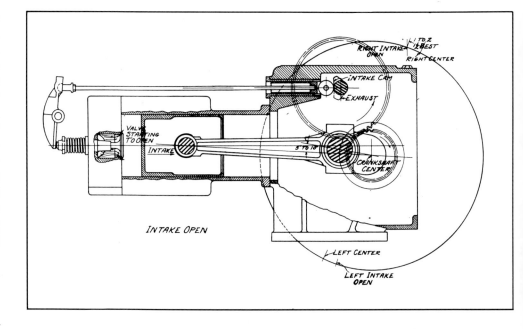

Hart-Parr 30
Drawing of the engine layout of the Hart-Parr 30.

Nichols & Shepard Company built steam traction engines for many years, as well as a line of conventional internal combustion tractors that was discontinued after the merger with Oliver. They introduced

Oliver Hart-Parr 18–28
The Model 18–28 was the first Oliver Hart-Parr to use a vertical engine, with the crankshaft lying parallel to the direction of travel. This example, built in 1935, is owned by the Pollisch Brothers of Ripon, Wisconsin. Although now on rubber, it was originally on steel.

their Red River Special line of threshers in 1902. The Battle Creek plant was used for producing threshers, harvesters, and other components until 1962, when White took over.

American Seeding Machine Company

The American Seeding Machine Company was the product of the merger craze that swept the country at the turn of the century. It was formed in 1903 from five companies, the oldest of which was founded in 1840. These were headed by the Superior Drill Company, Springfield, Ohio, and also included the Hoosier Drill Company, Bickford and Huffman, The Empire Drill Company, and Brennan and Company. Later, a sixth, A. C. Evans Company, was added.

The American Seeding Machine Company was a leader in developing planting equipment for dry-land and winter wheat areas. The plant remained in Springfield, Ohio, after the merger into Oliver, producing spreaders, cultivators, and planters until 1959.

Oliver Hart-Parr Tractors under Oliver

At the time of the merger, Hart-Parr had three tractors in production: the 12–24, 18–36, and 28–50.

Hart-Parr 12–24 "H"

This was an updated version of the 12–25 of 1918 that drove Hart and Parr from the company. It was a fairly capable and competitive standard-tread tractor. Remember that by

Hart-Parr 30 "A"
The Hart-Parr 30 was so influential in later tractor developments that it could not be overlooked. The full designation of this 1920 example was 15-30 "A." It was an outgrowth of the New Hart-Parr of 1918. Later in 1918, the bore was increased to 6.50in from 6.00in to bring the rating up from the original 12–25 drawbar and belt horsepower.

37

Previous page
Hart-Parr 30 "A"
Hart-Parr used two-cylinder side-by-side horizontal engines exclusively until 1923 when their first four-cylinder came out. This 1920 Model 30 used a typical Hart-Parr engine of the time. It employed cylinders with a 6.50in bore. The crankshaft had two throws, like the John Deere Waterloo Boy engines, but unlike the International Harvester Titans, which had both pistons on one throw. Like the Titan and Waterloo Boy, the cylinder heads of the 30 were to the rear; John Deere tractors had their cylinder heads forward.

1929, the Fordson was gone from the competitive scene and the new craze was for the all-purpose, or Farmall-type, tractor. The big players in the field were Case, Allis-Chalmers, John Deere, and International Harvester. Rubber tires were just beginning to be used on orchard tractors, and on October 29, 1929, the stock market crash sent the country into the worst depression in history.

The 12–24 "H" featured a two-cylinder, four-cycle, valve-in-head, 850rpm engine. Bore and stroke was 5.75x6.5in. The transmission provided two forward speeds. The

Hart-Parr 30 "A"
The exhaust of the New Hart-Parr comes out the front axle pivot point. This 1920 Hart-Parr 30, owned by David Preuhs of LeCenter, Minnesota, is equipped with a muffler. The printing on the front frame proclaims Hart-Parr to be the founders of the tractor industry, since their Charles City plant began producing tractors in 1902. Also, in 1906, the Hart-Parr sales manager is credited with coining the word "tractor" for use in advertising copy.

12–24 had a shipping weight of 4,800lb. Nebraska Test Number 129 (1926) indicated that the rating given the 12–24 rating was quite conservative, as the tractor was actually capable of a higher rating. A little-known fact about the 12–24 was that it could be equipped with an optional "live" power take-off (PTO), certainly the first in the industry.

Hart-Parr 18–36 "H"

This scaled up version of the 12–24 "H" was also quite a competitive and capable tractor for its day. It used a 6.75x7.0in bore and stroke, two-cylinder, four-cycle horizontal engine, and was rated to pull four 14in plow bottoms. Thus equipped, it could plow one acre per hour, no mean feat in those days. The 6,100lb Series "H" version, introduced in 1927, used a three-speed transmission, rather than the two-speed unit used in earlier versions.

Competition for the 18–36, which sold for about $1,350 in 1928, included the 8,000lb Huber Master Four 25–50 at about $3,000 and the 4,000lb John Deere Model D at $1,000, both of which claimed one acre per hour plowing capability.

Hart-Parr 28–50

An interesting variation on Hart-Parr's theme, this version used a four-cylinder, four-cycle engine that was in actuality, two 12–24 engines side-by-side. This monster had a shipping weight of 8,600lb and a working weight of more than 10,000lb, and recorded a pull of 7,347lb in Nebraska Test Number 140. The transmission provided two forward speeds. The 28–50 was

Hart-Parr 30 "A"
The engine of this New Hart-Parr is a two-cylinder, four-stroke type. The carburetor is the Dray kerosene shunt, an exclusive product of Hart-Parr Company, which automatically supplied the engine with heated fuel on light loads and cold fuel on heavy loads.

Hart-Parr 30 "A"
The friction drive for the Hart-Parr 30's fan and water pump shaft. Hart-Parr was one of the first to get away from gravity water circulation systems. This 1920 example is owned by David Preuhs of LeCenter, Minnesota.

rated for six 14in bottoms or a 36in threshing machine. In 1928, it sold for a bit over $2,000, which included an open-air cab and fenders.

These three tractor models that were in production by Hart-Parr when the merger took place in 1929 were continued through the 1930 model year. Despite dire economic times, work was continued on three replacement models for introduction

during the 1930 model year: the 18–27, 18–28, and 28–44. With these, the Hart-Parr name was displayed prominently, but a small "Oliver" was added above or below it.

**Oliver Hart-Parr 18–27
1930–1937**
Beginning with this tractor and all others that followed under the Oliver name, a conventional vertical engine was used, and the crankshaft was longitudinal, rather than transverse. The 18–27 was Oliver's answer to the Farmall. It was a row-crop machine of the finest tradition, featuring a single front wheel and good clearance under the drive

Next page
Hart-Parr 16–30
This Hart-Parr 16–30 is of 1926 vintage, an improved version of the Model 30. Weighing 6,000lb for Nebraska Test Number 106, the 16–30 exerted a maximum pull of 4,913lb. Attesting to the conservativeness of the Hart-Parr Company, maximum observed belt and drawbar horsepowers were 37 and 25, respectively. The 16–30 used a Stromberg MB-3 carburetor, rather than the Dray. Also available for the 16–30 was the new United Whirling Vane dry air cleaner. This nicely-restored tractor is owned by David Preuhs of LeCenter, Minnesota.

LEFT SIDE VIEW OF HART-PARR 16-30

Hart-Parr 16–30

In the days before the Oliver-Hart-Parr merger, Hart-Parr's mainstay tractor was the 16–30 designed to pull three to four plows.

axles. Cultivating and planting equipment were mountable forward of the rear wheels, where the operator had a good view. The 18–27 was the first to use the skeleton "tip-toe" rear wheels.

Hart-Parr 22–40

The Hart-Parr 22–40 was powered by two Hart-Parr 12–24 cylinder blocks placed side by side.

LEFT SIDE VIEW OF HART-PARR 22–40 SHOWING DIRECT DRIVEN BELT PULLEY, ALSO ACCESSIBLE TRANSMISSION AND CLUTCH CONSTRUCTION

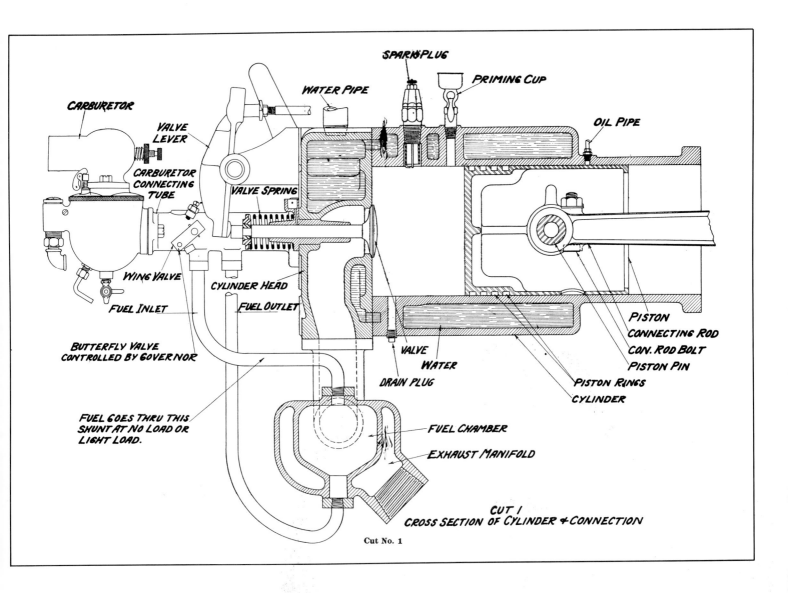

CARBURETOR

VALVE LEVER

CARBURETOR CONNECTING TUBE

VALVE SPRING

WING VALVE

FUEL INLET

CYLINDER HEAD

FUEL OUTLET

BUTTERFLY VALVE CONTROLLED BY GOVERNOR

FUEL GOES THRU THIS SHUNT AT NO LOAD OR LIGHT LOAD.

WATER PIPE

SPARK PLUG

PRIMING CUP

OIL PIPE

PISTON

CONNECTING ROD

CON. ROD BOLT

PISTON PIN

PISTON RINGS

CYLINDER

VALVE

WATER

DRAIN PLUG

FUEL CHAMBER

EXHAUST MANIFOLD

CUT 1
CROSS SECTION OF CYLINDER & CONNECTION

Cut No. 1

The engine for the 18–27 was a four-cylinder, valve-in-head type, with a bore and stroke of 4.13x5.25in and an operating speed of 1190rpm. Shipping weight of the tractor was only 4,100lb, and the operating weight could be around 4,600lb, making the 18–27 comparable to the very successful Farmall. The 18–27 was tested at the University of Nebraska in April 1930 under Test Number 176. In later years (it was produced until 1937), it was available with a dual narrow front and rubber tires.

Oliver Hart-Parr 18–28 1930–1937

This was essentially the standard-tread version of the 18–27; the same

engine, transmission, and differential combination was used, and the advertised speeds were the same in the gears despite different rear wheel sizes. It weighed 4,420lb when tested in July 1930 at the University of Nebraska, under Test Number 180. The 18–28 did not have the adjustable rear wheel spacing or the individual wheel brakes of the 18–27.

The 18–28 was also available in Orchard, Rice, and Western versions, and was sold in Canada as the Cockshutt Hart-Parr 18–28.

Oliver Hart-Parr 28–44 1930–1937

Successor to the Hart-Parr 18–36, this tractor began life as the Oliver

Hart-Parr 30
Cross-section drawing of the cylinder head and fuel flow for the Hart-Parr 30.

Hart-Parr Model A. After about 100 were sold, it was submitted to the University of Nebraska for testing, and then was given the 28–44 rating and designation. It later became known as the Oliver 90 and the Cockshutt 90. Still later, it became the 99. It was also sold in several industrial versions, some with six-cylinder engines.

The 28–44 was a big four- or five-plow machine, using a four-cylinder 443ci kerosene-burning valve-in-head engine with a bore and stroke of 4.75x6.25in. Operating speed was

Hart-Parr 12–24 "E"
The Hart-Parr 12–24 was produced as the "E" model between1924 and 1928. An "H" model 12–24, built from 1928 to 1930, was the same except for a 0.25in bore increase and a three-speed, rather than a two-speed, transmission.

Hart-Parr 12–24 "E"
The Hart-Parr 12–24 "E" was an improvement of the older 10–20 model. This 1927 example, owned by David Preuhs of Le Center, Minnesota, has what has to be one of the world's first live PTO. The shaft comes directly from the clutch-end of the engine, through a separate clutch, angling back across the platform through a series of universal joints.

Hart-Parr 12–24 "E"
The drive system for the water pump, magneto and the Madison-Kipp oiler of the Hart-Parr 12–24 are shown in this photo. The Hart-Parr 12–24 "E" featured a two-cylinder engine with a 5.50in diameter bore.

1125rpm. The transmission had three forward speeds. Operating weight during Nebraska Test Number 183, in October 1930, was 6,415lb. Almost 9,000 were sold, at an average price of $1,325.

The Great Depression
The early 1930s brought many changes. With the coming of the

Great Depression in Fall 1929, came a severe drought in the Great Plains. The once-prosperous wheat-producing lands were largely abandoned. As the Depression spread, farm income dropped worldwide. Tractor production plummeted. In 1932, tractor sales in the United States dropped to around 19,000 units, the fewest since 1915. This had a bigger "shaking-out" effect among manufacturers than was ever caused by competition with the Fordson. Of the forty-seven tractor makers left after the Great Tractor War of the twenties, only seven of any substance remained to produce wheel-

type farm tractors in 1933: International Harvester, Deere & Company, J. I. Case Company, Massey-Harris Company, Oliver Farm Equipment Company, Minneapolis-Moline Power Implement Company, and Allis-Chalmers Company.

The year 1934 saw a 40 percent increase in tractor sales over those of 1933, so the survivors were optimistic. Research and development continued unabated. In addition to the continued trend toward row-crop tractors, two other big changes were occurring.

The first was the slow move to pneumatic tires. The story begins in

1871, when a Thompson Rubber Tired Steamer was entered into the California State Fair. It was not a pneumatic tired tractor, using instead rubber blocks like cleats around both the front and rear wheels. Nothing much more happened until around 1928, when Florida citrus growers sought a solution to tree root damage caused by tractor cleats. They modified their steel rear wheels to mount discarded truck tire casings (without inner tubes), sometimes placing as many as three casings side-by-side on each wheel. The casings were mounted such that the natural strength in the curved rubber was enough to support the tractor without pneumatics. These "tires" provided both flotation

and traction, and proved so successful that the attention of the major tire companies was attracted.

In 1931, the B. F. Goodrich Company brought out its Zero Pressure tire for tractors, which was on the same concept as the improvised citrus grower tire. These "rubber arch" tires provided more traction than either solid rubber or early tractor pneumatics.

Allis-Chalmers engineers began experimenting with low-pressure pneumatic tires in 1930, and two years later, fitted an A-C Model U with a pair of Firestone airplane tires on the rear. Later that year, Allis-Chalmers announced that rubber tires would be standard equipment for the Model U. The Model U

Hart-Parr 28-50
The Hart-Parr 28-50 was more after the fashion of the early Hart-Parrs: the weight of this tractor approached 5 tons. The four-cylinder engine had a bore and stroke of 5.75x6.50in and operated at 850rpm and was essentially two 12–24 engines side-by-side. It could pull a six-bottom plow or operate a 36in threshing machine.

was then equipped with a "road gear," giving it a top speed of around 10mph. If you ordered your Model U on steel, the road gear was locked out.

Nevertheless, farmers of the early-thirties were reluctant to give up their steel wheels and cleats—main-

Oliver Hart-Parr 18–27
The Brothers Pollesch, Southern Wisconsin tractor collectors, own this nice 1932 Oliver Hart-Parr 18–27 Dual. The vertical four-cylinder engine and the transmission of the 18–27 were the same as those used in the standard-tread 18–28. Built between 1931 and 1937, it was the forerunner of the Oliver 80.

ly because they had had poor experience with pneumatic tires on their cars and trucks, but also because of the economic times; most farmers were struggling to keep their land and were in no mood to experiment with newfangled ideas.

Accordingly, to dissuade the skepticism, the tire and tractor companies staged plowing and speed con-

Oliver Hart-Parr 18–28
Beginning in 1930 with the Model 18–28, the logo featured a big "Oliver" and a smaller "Hart-Parr." Also with this model, the Madison-Kipp oiler system was gone, replaced with a more modern and conventional oil pan and pump under the crankshaft. Almost 4,000 of these tractors were built before production was discontinued in 1937. The 18–28 was essentially the standard-tread version of the 18–27 row-crop.

tests. On September 17, 1933, Barney Oldfield drove a stock A-C Model U with a special road gear to a world speed record of 64.28mph.

By the 1934 model year, all the leading manufacturers were offering rubber-tired tractors. Of the wheel-type tractors sold in 1935, 14 per-

Previous page
Oliver Hart-Parr 28–44
Built between 1930 and 1937, the Oliver Hart-Parr 28–44 was the forerunner of the Oliver 90. It was a big four- to five-plow machine with a 443ci engine and a three-speed transmission. The tractor shown was seen at the 1992 Midwest Thresherman's Reunion near Pontiac, Illinois. *Robert N. Pripps*

cent were mounted on rubber; that figure rose to 31 percent by 1936 and 95 percent by 1940. The early years of World War II saw a return to steel wheels, as rubber was a critical war effort material.

The second major development in the early 1930s was in fuels. Kerosene had become the fuel of choice for agriculture since its use was pioneered by Hart-Parr. This

Oliver Hart-Parr Model A
This 1930 Oliver Hart-Parr Model A is owned by David Pruehs of Le Center, Minnesota. The Model A later became the 28–44, after it had been tested at the University of Nebraska. Still later, it evolved into the 90 and the 99. This tractor was featured as the January tractor in the 1992 Dupont calender and in their video.

was due, in part, to the great price disparity between kerosene and gasoline (10–15¢ per gallon), but there were other factors as well. Gasoline evaporated, it was more dangerous to store, it had less energy per pound, and it was inconsistent in quality.

The rise in acceptance of the automobile was forcing some rethinking of gasoline, however, because it was in such common use therein. And, despite the claimed advantages of kerosene, it did have some disadvantages.

Being a fairly nonvolatile liquid, vaporization of kerosene in the carburetor and manifold was a challenge to the engine designers. Since heat was required, almost all kerosene tractors were started on gasoline and then switched over to kerosene when warm. This meant that gasoline had to be kept around the place anyway.

Furthermore, the extra energy per pound in kerosene was causing a problem, rather than being an advantage. To keep from generating destructive heat during the combustion process, compression ratios were necessarily lower. Excess fuel was also metered in by the carburetor to act as a cooling agent. In addition, in hot weather, water was added to the inlet air for additional combustion chamber cooling. The result was that a kerosene tractor with a given engine displacement used about 25 percent more fuel than a corresponding gasoline tractor and produced about 10 percent less work. This advantage of gasoline was not true of a kerosene tractor being run on gasoline, but only on a tractor

Oliver Hart-Parr Model A
The Oliver Hart-Parr Model A, forerunner of the 28–44, had a four-cylinder 443ci engine with a 4.75x6.25in bore and stroke. The engine had a rated operating speed of 1125rpm. It was a Waukesha design, but was completely built at Charles City, including the block casting.

with an engine designed to take full advantage of gasoline.

Finally, spurred on by the large demands of the automobile industry, fuel companies began to take the quality of their gasolines seriously. The invention of tetraethyl lead also did much to allow fuel companies to standardize octane ratings of gasolines. By 1934, regular gasoline motor fuel had standardized on an octane rating of seventy. This rating allowed a compression ratio of 6.0:1 or 6.5:1 without detonation problems. Kerosene engines were relegated to a nominal 4.0:1. Fuel companies began experimenting with improved kerosene-based (distillate) fuels, increasing their volatility and decreasing their heat content. Eventually marketed was a "tractor fuel" which could operate with 5.0:1 compression ratios.

A Change in Direction: Oliver Hart-Parr 70 1935–1937

This tractor marked one of the most profound turning points in the farm implement industry's direction. It reflected both the optimism of the improving economic situation and the increasing influence of the automobile on tractor design. In 1933–1935, durable goods compa-

Oliver Hart-Parr 70 Row Crop
Roger Pollesch guides his 1936 Oliver Hart-Parr 70 Row Crop along the edge of a field. The skeleton, or "Tip-Toe," wheels were an Oliver feature. These wheels provided superior traction in most soil conditions, but if the tractor was stalled, they would instantly dig deep holes.

nies were beginning to see that styling and product differentiation had a positive effect on sales. Until the 1930s, cars, for example, were quite a bit alike: boxy, four-cylinders, clam fenders, exposed radiators. By the mid-1930s, styling was

55

individualistic. Six-, eight-, twelve-, and even sixteen-cylinder engines had replaced the fours, and radiator grilles were the hallmark of styling.

Although there had been some attempts at tractor styling before, the new Oliver 70, in 1935, was so car-like that it immediately overshadowed the competition. It influenced tractor design from then on. It was styled, it was powered by a six-cylinder engine, it could be equipped with an electric starter and lights, its high-compression engine was designed to run on 70-octane (hence the model designation) gasoline, and it had an instrument panel and fingertip controls. Advertising of the day showed "Sister" and "Bud" taking their turns at the wheel.

The Oliver 70 (now with a big "Oliver" and a smaller "Hart-Parr") was available in four configurations: row-crop, standard-tread, orchard, and high-crop. Each configuration offered the option of the HC (high-compression) gasoline engine or the KD (kerosene-distillate) engine; both were six-cylinder engines. It was also sold in Canada as the Cockshutt 70.

The smooth six-cylinder power was ideal for belt work. The 70 could handle a 22x36 thresher with ease. Oliver claimed an optimistic one-acre-per-hour plowing rate: quite an accomplishment for a 3,000lb tractor with only a bit over 200ci displacement. (Bore and stroke was 3.13x4.38in, and operating speed was 1500rpm.)

A four-speed transmission was provided for the row-crop versions, and six-speed units were provided for the standard-tread and orchard

versions. With the latter two, road speeds of 14mph were possible.

Other features of the 70 were a high-pressure engine oil system, water pump, magneto ignition, muffler, differential (steering) brakes, and adjustable wheel spacing (row-crops). Finally, while rubber tires were not standard on the 70, Oliver pushed them hard, even offering special discounts if both steel and rubber were ordered with the tractor.

One of the most interesting innovations associated with the Oliver 70 of 1935 was the "Tractor Color Voting Contest." The idea was to draw attention to the tractor at county fairs, and to find out what color scheme was preferred by potential customers. Six striking combinations were shown, and some were sold to customers as painted: chrome green body with red trim and ivory lettering; regatta red body, aluminum trim, and white lettering; chrome green body, tangerine trim, and white lettering; yellow body, black trim, and red lettering; China gold body, tangerine trim, and ivory lettering; ivory body, China gold trim, and red lettering. As a result of the voting, the first combination was chosen.

Oliver Hart-Parr 70 Row Crop
With the introduction of the 70 Series, the "Hart-Parr" was smaller in the logo than the "Oliver." The 70 was available in row-crop, orchard, and standard-tread versions. Each of these could be obtained in the KD version for kerosene or the HC (high compression) version for use with 70 octane gasoline. Pictured is a 1936 70 Row Crop owned by the Pollesch Brothers of Ripon Wisconsin.

Chapter 5

Oliver Tractors

In automobiles, streamlines have followed
the development of high compression motors;
new beauty symbolized new, smooth power.
—Oliver advertising copy

With the 1938 model year, the Hart-Parr name was dropped from the tractors, although there was still much reference to it in trade literature. The 1938 models were introduced in October 1937, as Oliver continued to relate its tractors to the automobile (next-year's models being announced in the Fall). There were two newly restyled models and two models that were upgraded carryovers from previous production.

Oliver marketing people had felt like the tail-wagging-the-dog since the 70 of 1935 had gotten the jump

Oliver 70 Orchard
This view clearly shows the clean lines of Everett Jensen's 1945 Oliver 70 Orchard. As a young man, Jensen worked as an Oliver and International Harvester mechanic, eventually (some thirty-five years ago now) opening an automotive service station in Clarks Grove, Minnesota. He gradually moved into the small engine and lawn equipment business and out of the automotive area. He became a Polaris dealer in 1969. Everett's wife, Dianne, was basically a city girl, but her dad farmed with Oliver tractors prior to moving into town.

Henry Ford and Ford 9N
A dapper Henry Ford doffs his farmer's straw hat after giving a plowing demonstration of his new 9N Ford-Ferguson. The eight-year-old boy, standing by the tractor, next mounted the driver's seat and gave a plowing demonstration of his own. The results were as good as those of the experienced plowman Ford. The occasion was the tractor's press introduction in June 1939.

Previous page
Oliver Cletrac Model HG
Oliver bought the Cleveland Tractor Company (Cletrac) in 1944 and continued production of its line of crawler tractors under the name Oliver Cletrac. The Model HG was introduced by Cletrac in 1939. It weighed a little over 4,000lb and was powered by an L-head Hercules four-cylinder engine of 3.25x4.00in bore and stroke. This tractor, thought to be a 1952 model by its owners, the Pollesch Brothers, is equipped with Cletrac's patented push-type cultivator. The cultivator is of the mechanical-lift, or "Armstrong," variety.

on the competition, but 1938 and 1939 were to be watershed years for the industry. Both John Deere and International Harvester had retained the services of world-renowned stylists; their tractors were to be modernized in ways other than looks.

The biggest impact, however, was to come from Henry Ford. In June 1939, Ford introduced the famous Ford-Ferguson 9N, and the tractor world has not been the same since. The feature that made the 9N so special was the hydraulic three-point hitch, brought in by agreement with Harry Ferguson, of Ireland. With the Ferguson system (the hitch and custom implements), the 2,500lb, $600 Ford-Ferguson 9N could outperform tractors weighing and costing twice as much. The Ford-Ferguson also established the trend away from the row-crop configuration and toward

Oliver Cletrac Model HG
Rollin White founded the Cleveland Motor Plow Company in1917. White, of sewing machine and steam car fame, renamed the company Cleveland Tractor Company, or Cletrac, for short. Cletrac was one of the first to offer diesels, beginning in 1933. The tractors were rather stark and functional in appearance, until styled in 1937 by industrial designer Lawrence Blazey. While Author Pripps was growing up, his father had several Cletracs at his Wisconsin Conservation Department Ranger Station.

the high-axle wide-front, or "utility," configuration.

Most in the tractor industry thought the new Ford was just another Fordson and didn't take it seriously. When sales for its first full year of production topped 35,000, however, they knew they had to react. In this, Oliver was at a disadvantage, having reconfigured its tractors before the impact of the competition was known. Although Oliver had a "motor-lift" for implements, it would be after World War II before hydraulics would be incorporated. Although Oliver never quite recovered from this loss of competitive momentum, the tractors it produced during these next years were among the finest and best performing of the world's farm machines.

The Fleetline Series: Oliver 70 1937–1948

The restyled 70 introduced the Oliver Fleetline Series. Under the sheet metal, the 70 was essentially the same as before. It was available in the row-crop configuration, with either dual or single front wheels, standard-tread, orchard, and industrial models. These tractors were sold in Canada in Cockshutt livery. There was also an interesting variation, the Airport 25, an especially modified 70 standard-tread for airport use. Standard equipment included the electrical system, both hand and foot brakes, front and rear drawbars, and a side exhaust.

The American Society of Agricultural Engineers (ASAE) proposed standards for hitch and PTO locations and for PTO shields. Oliver incorporated these items for the 1939 models of the 70. Rubber tires and the six-speed transmission were also made standard.

Oliver 80 1937–1948

The Oliver 80 was an agricultural variation of the Oliver Hart-Parr 80 industrial model, which was, in turn, based on the old Hart-Parr

Get things done with an OLIVER!

● Power when you want it—power when you need it—power to help put in crops when field conditions are right and time and help are limited—that's the power you'll find in an Oliver Row Crop 60 or 70.

In the Oliver 70, you have a husky, high compression, six-cylinder engine that really buckles down when the going gets tough. It's the smoothest power ever built into a tractor.

The Oliver 60 has *big tractor* features—with an engine stout enough to handle most farming operations—plowing, planting, cultivating, harvesting. Like the 70, it has the famous Fuel Miser, the governor that measures out only the fuel needed—not too much, not too little.

Pep up your farm work with an Oliver Row Crop—and save time with Oliver's new "QD" (Quick-Detachable) system of hooking up tractor-mounted tools. But you better see your Oliver dealer now. Limited production means that there may not be enough to go around.

The OLIVER Corporation
400 West Madison Street, Chicago 6, Illinois

★ ★ ★

Here's the watchdog that guards fuel consumption —the famous Fuel Miser that gives cylinders only the fuel they need for maximum efficiency.

THE FINEST IN FARM MACHINERY

18–27 and 18–28. When introduced for the 1938 model year, it was available with either a high-compression gasoline engine or a kerosene-distillate engine. It was also available in either standard-tread or row-crop models. These tractors were un-

Oliver advertisement
The new Row Crop 70 with Oliver's streamlined bodywork design.

Previous page
Oliver 70 Orchard
Everett Jensen's 1945 Oliver Orchard looks like it would have been at home in the Indianapolis 500. The graceful fenders allowed the machine to work between the trees.

styled, appearing much the same as the earlier version.

The power outputs for the gasoline and kerosene versions were about the same. The kerosene version had a maximum brake horsepower of 37.03, while that of the gasoline version was 38.11—not enough difference to notice. For the kerosene version, however, the bore was increased to 4.50in, compared to 4.25in for the gasoline engine. The original 18–28 used a bore of 4.125in. The stroke for all three was 5.25in. Nebraska Tests for the 80s were Numbers 300, 301, and 365.

For the 1939 model year, ASAE-standardized PTO and hitch configurations were incorporated, as was a four-speed transmission for the 80. For the 1940 year model, Oliver introduced an 80 Diesel, equipped with a Buda-Lanova engine. The

Oliver 70 Orchard
The engine cover has been removed from this 1945 Oliver 70 Orchard to expose the neatly packaged six-cylinder engine. Note the muffler was above the manifold, with the exhaust exiting the hole in the hood. Non-Orchard models had a length of exhaust pipe sticking straight up above the hood.

Lanova combustion chamber/injection design dated back to 1927 by Franz Lang, an associate of Rudolf Diesel.

With 14in bottoms, the Oliver 80 was considered a three-plow tractor.

Oliver 90 1937–1953

This tractor was a modernized version of the old 28–44, or Model A. It was also sold as the Cockshutt 90. The same four-cylinder, 4.75x6.25in bore and stroke, 1125rpm engine was used, but it was improved with high-pressure lubrication, a self starter, and a centrifugal governor. Both kerosene and gasoline versions were available, but the engine was not of the high-compression type. The tractor featured a four-speed transmission and an optional PTO.

After 1952, when production was moved from Charles City to South Bend, some 90s were built with six-cylinder engines.

Oliver 60 1940–1948

By 1940, Oliver was feeling the competitive pressure of the Ford-Ferguson and the school of other lightweight tractors that had come on the market since 1938. Foremost of these were the Farmall A, the John Deere H, and the Allis-Chalmers B. Farmers were getting serious about completely replacing

Oliver 70 Row Crop

Everett Jensen of Clarks Grove, Minnesota, obtained this 1944 single-front-wheel Oliver 70 Row Crop in the Montezuma, Iowa, area. It's serial number 254618. The former owner used it in vegetable and sugar beet growing. The Oliver 70 Standard (for standard tread) is essentially the same as the Row Crop wide-front, except it is lower, the front wheel axle mounting is under the radiator, rather than in front of it, and adjustable wheel spacing is not provided.

their horses with mechanical power, and these small tractors offered the low cost and maneuverability needed.

Oliver introduced the 60, which looked like an 8/10 scale model of the 70, with a four-cylinder, 3.30x3.50in (bore and stroke), 1500rpm engine. Both gasoline and distillate versions were available. The 60 was the last of the "old" Fleetlines. It was available in row-crop, standard-tread, and industrial versions. Rubber tires were standard equipment, but during the war years, many were sold on steel. A four-speed transmission was used. Some were equipped with distributor-type ignitions, and some with Wico magnetos. The 60 came with individual rear wheel brakes and an optional electrical system.

The Oliver 60, which was sold in Canada as the Cockshutt 60 until 1946, was tested at the University of Nebraska in Test Number 375 in September 1941.

The Double-Numbered Series: Oliver 99 1937–1957

One of the most successful of the Oliver line, the 99 had the longest production run of any Oliver tractor. It actually had its beginning in 1932 as the 99 Industrial Special High-Compression. As such, several agricultural variations were sold as the Riceland and the Thresherman's Special. For the 1938 model year, a strictly agricultural 99 was offered. Production of the 99 was moved from Charles City to the South Bend plant in 1952.

Cockshutt 80

Grandmaster tractor collector Walter Kellor of Forest Junction, Wisconsin, owns this pristine Cockshutt 80. The tractor was restored by Doug Grantvroot of Clear Lake, South Dakota. It is essentially the same as the Oliver 80, which had its beginnings as the 18–28. The engine is a four-cylinder unit capable of burning either kerosene, or with high compression heads, 70-plus octane gasoline.

The 99 replaced the 90 after it had one year of production at the South Bend plant. The 99 was originally configured for 70 octane gasoline, but after the move to South Bend, six-cylinder gasoline and diesel engines were added. The original four-cylinder, 443ci gasoline engine was identical to that of the 90, except for the high-compression head. The six-cylinder engine boasted 302ci, with a 6.25:1 compression ratio for gasoline and 15.5:1 for the Lavona combustion-chamber diesel. It was essentially the same engine as used in the Oliver 88.

After the move to South Bend, styling was also added to the 99. It was available in standard-tread and Ricefield models, only.

The 99 was a big tractor by any comparison, with a base weight of 7,500lb. Operating weights could approach 11,000lb. In Nebraska Test Number 451, the 99 produced nearly 60hp on the belt. The 99 was sold in Canada as the Cockshutt 99 until 1953.

Oliver 88 1947–1954

To commemorate Oliver's 100th anniversary, a new series of tractors was announced in the fall of 1947 for the 1948 model year, and the Oliver 60, 70, and 80 were replaced by the new Fleetline 66, 77, and 88. Standardization was a key item with these new tractors, especially regarding interchangeability among the models. All models were available with distillate or gasoline engines, while the 88 was offered in a six-cylinder diesel from the beginning. Almost all had six-speed (two reverses) transmissions, and all had thermostatically controlled cooling systems. Three row-crop versions of each were offered: dual narrow-front, single front wheel, and ad-

Cockshutt 99 and a Oliver Hart-Parr 80
A Cockshutt 99 and a Oliver Hart-Parr 80 stand together at the 1992 Midwest Thresherman's Reunion near Pontiac, Illinois. *Robert N. Pripps*

Oliver 60 Row Crop
An Oliver 60 Row Crop (wide-front) owned by the Mitchell Brothers of Fulton, Michigan. The 60 used a four-cylinder engine producing a maximum belt horsepower of 18.4. In the background is a 1936 Oliver Hart-Parr.

justable wide-front. Standard-tread, orchard, industrial, and high-crop versions were also available in most models.

It should be noted that 88s built in 1947 and early 1948, before the 100th anniversary, retained the old Fleetline styling. This is especially unusual since the Model 80s were unstyled.

The Oliver 88 was rated to handle four 14in plows. The row-crop version had adjustable wheel spacing, while the standard-tread type did not. The 231ci, six-cylinder engine used a bore and stroke of 3.50x4.00in for the diesel and gasoline versions. The kerosene-distillate engine used a bore of 3.75in, giving a displacement of 265ci. Compression ratios for the engines were as follows: gasoline, 6.75:1; distillate, 4.75:1; and diesel, 15.5:1. Rated en-

gine speed was 1600rpm for all versions. The new Hydra-Lectric hydraulic implement lift system was added in 1949.

Oliver 77 1947–1954

The Oliver 77 was originally available with either the gasoline or the kerosene-distillate engine. In 1949, a diesel engine replaced the kerosene-distillate, and in 1952, a liquefied petroleum gas version of the HC engine was added. All were six-cylinders.

Displacements and other facts for the 77 engine options follow:

Model	Displacement	Bore	Stroke	Compression	RPM
HC gas & LPG	194ci	3.31in	3.75in	6.75:1	1600
Kerosene-distillate	216ci	3.50in	3.75in	4.75:1	1600
Diesel	194ci	3.31in	3.75in	15.5:1	1600

The 77 was considered a three-bottom tractor, using 14in plows. In 1949, the Hydra-Lectric hydraulic lift system was an added option, providing either electric or manual control of attached implements.

Oliver 66 1947–1954

The nifty little 66 used the same configuration engines as the 77, except they were four-cylinder, rather than six-cylinder types. Displacements were: gasoline, 129ci; kerosene-distillate, 144ci; liquefied petroleum gas, 129ci; and diesel, 129ci. Hydraulics were also available on the 66.

The Super Series: Oliver Super 55 1954–1958

In 1951, Oliver sold approximately 25,000 wheel-type agricultural

Oliver 88

The first of the new Fleetline Series, the Oliver 88 was built between 1947 and 1954. Introduced as 1948 models, the new Fleetline Series also included the 66 and 77. The smart new styling and other improvements celebrated Oliver's 100th year. The 231ci six-cylinder engine enabled the 88 to pull a four-bottom plow. Kerosene, gasoline, and diesel versions were available, although the kerosene version had a displacement of 265ci. Kerosene tractor engines were often made larger in displacement to offset the loss of power resulting from the lower compression ratio required for kerosene. This 1952 Model 88 is owned by the Pollesch Brothers as their "pulling tractor." Bore and stroke are standard, but M&W domed pistons are used.

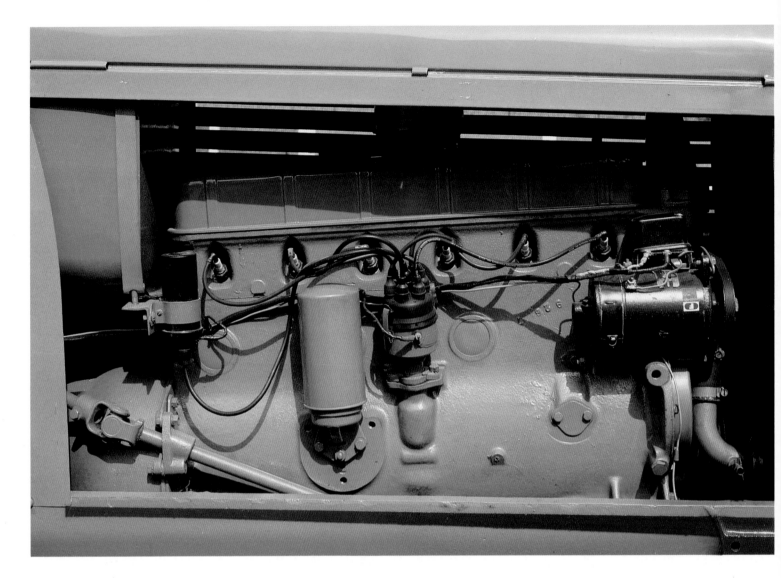

Oliver 88
The Oliver 88 was powered by a smooth-running six-cylinder engine governed at 1600rpm. Shown is a 1948 model with the engine side panel removed. Note how the steering shaft proceeds alongside the engine through a series of universal joints.

tractors of all sizes. Ford sold 98,400 of its single model, the 8N, during the same period. Oliver management concluded that the utility tractor and the three-point hitch were here to stay and that they should look into a version of their own. Thus was born the Super 55 for introduction in the 1954 model year. Missing no options, Oliver management made the Super 55 look like the

Ford and sit like the Ford; it was even styled like the Ford.

The dissolution of the agreement between Ford and Ferguson in 1947, and the resulting lawsuit settlement in 1952, made the patent situation of the load-compensating three-point hitch somewhat clouded. When Young Henry Ford took over from his grandfather in 1946, he soon recognized that Harry Ferguson was making all the money on their agreement. He therefore told Ferguson that as of mid-1947, the agreement was dissolved.

With that, Ford set about revising and improving the tractor from the Ford-Ferguson into the Ford 8N (the "8" signifying model year 1948). He then set up his own dealer network

(previously, it had been Ferguson's), and built a complete line of three-point hitch implements (these, too, had been Ferguson's). Ferguson countered by launching his own U.S. tractor, the TO-20; importing his TE-20 (already in production in England); and suing Ford for loss of business and patent infringement.

The lawsuit settlement made it clear to the other tractor companies that Ferguson's patents could be circumvented. In the early-Thirties, Harry Ferguson had developed and patented what he called "Draft Control." In his concept, the upper link (sometimes called the "free-link") pushed forward on a hydraulic control valve in proportion to the rear-ward, or draft load, on the imple-

Oliver 88
The left-hand view of the Oliver 88's six-cylinder engine. The smooth, even power of the big six became an Oliver trademark, in stark contrast to the two-cylinder engine of the competitive John Deere Model G. Both tractors, however, have equally diehard supporters and enjoy similar successes at antique tractor pulls.

ment. Once the hand-operated hydraulic control positioned the implement to the desired depth setting, the free-link manipulated the hy-

draulics, raising or lowering the implement as required to keep draft load constant.

When set up properly, the three-point hitch made plowing an absolute snap. When the Ford-Ferguson was first introduced to the press in 1939, a plowing demonstration was given by an eight-year old boy! Even in small fields, the 120ci, 2,500lb Ford could plow one acre per hour.

The Oliver Super 55 was one of the first of the new breed of utility tractors with the three-point hitch to hit the market. It featured a 144ci,

Next page
Oliver 77 Standard
Oliver's three-plow 77 Standard shows off its New Fleetline Styling. The new styling was in commemoration of Oliver's 100th year anniversary. This one, a 1948 model, is owned by the Pollesch Brothers of Ripon, Wisconsin.

four-cylinder Oliver engine powered by either gasoline or diesel fuel. Bore and stroke was 3.50x3.75in. Governed speed was 2000rpm. The compression ratio for the gasoline version was 7:1, a new high for trac-

Oliver 77 Standard

The instrument panel of the 1948 Oliver 77 was rather Spartan. The tag to the right of the instruments shows the double-H shift pattern for the six-speed transmission.

Oliver 77 Row Crop

Features of the Oliver 77 Row Crop included a rubber torsion spring seat, a "live" PTO, and the Hydra-Lectric implement control system.

tors, a factor improving fuel economy. Also used was a six-speed transmission, providing a road speed of almost 15mph. In first gear, rate of travel could be as low as 0.75mph.

Oliver Super 66 1954–1958

Using the same four-cylinder engines and transmission as the Super 55, the Super 66 replaced the 66. The three-point hitch was available, but with the Hydra-Lectric hydraulic lift system. Standard-tread and row-crop versions were available, as was, for the first time, an adjustable wide-front row-crop.

An interesting feature of the Super 66 was its three-setting governor. The engine operated at 1600rpm for PTO work, 1750rpm for drawbar work, and 2000rpm for belt work. This was necessary to accom-

modate existing gear designs from both strength and ratio standpoints.

Credit is due Oliver for two things it pioneered at this time: the small diesel and the twelve-volt electrical system. By 1958, Oliver built 90 percent of all diesel farm tractors. It was 1960 before some of the other manufacturers went to twelve-volt electrical systems. Even Oliver was somewhat slow in adopting the alternator to replace the traditional brush-type generator.

Oliver Super 77 1954–1958

Replacing the Oliver 77, the Super 77 was a three- or four-plow tractor. The Super 77 was available in all the 77's configurations, plus the new adjustable wide-front row-crop. A Hydra-Lectric three-point hitch was available on all versions. Also new for the Super 77s was a

Previous page
Oliver 66 Row Crop
A 1951 model Oliver Row Crop 66. With its six-speed transmission, live PTO, and its neat styling, it competed well with the Ford 8N, Farmall H, Case VAC, and the Massey-Harris 22.

new front frame for the row-crop versions, allowing drive-in mounting of cultivators, planters, and other implements.

The Super 77 used the same engine as the Super 55 and Super 66, except it had six, instead of four, cylinders. The engine was governed at 1600rpm. Gasoline, diesel, and liquefied petroleum gas versions were available for each type of tractor, including orchard, row-crop, high-crop, industrial, and standard-tread.

Oliver Super 88 1954–1958

Advertised as the most powerful tractor in its class, the Super 88 was the first Oliver row-crop to top 50hp as a drawbar rating. The 3.75x4.00in bore and stroke, 265ci engine, operating at 1600rpm, was retained from the old 88 kerosene-distillate, which was dropped in favor of the diesel.

Oliver Super 55 Diesel
George and Jo Ann Lulich have this completely restored 1955 Oliver Super 55 Diesel on their farm near Mason, Wisconsin. The Super 55 is a utility-type tractor with a four-cylinder engine, a six-speed (two reverse) transmission, live PTO and hydraulics, and a three-point hitch. It has a twelve-volt electrical system and uses two six-volt batteries.

Next page
Oliver Super 66 Diesel
In the 1950s, Oliver produced more than 90 percent of the diesel farm tractors. This 1966 Super 66 Diesel, owned by Charlie Lulich of Mason, Wisconsin, was restored from a basket case. It was painted by George Bizub. Charlie, pictured on the tractor, is only its second owner.

Previous page
Oliver Super 77 Diesel
Roger Pollesch starts his brother Ken's Oliver Super 77 Diesel for the Father's Day 1992 photo session; note the puff of smoke from the exhaust. This Super 77 is a 1955 model. Engine side covers were not used on the Oliver Super Series tractors.

The compression ratio of the gasoline version was upped to 7.0:1.

The Super 88 shared other features of the Super Series, including, for the first time on Oliver styled tractors, no engine-covering side panels.

Oliver Super 99 1955–1958
The Super 99 was the sixth in the Super Series of Oliver tractors. It

Oliver Super 77 Diesel
A wood bundle wagon with an oak frame stands by Ken Pollesch's 1955 Oliver Super 77 Diesel. Fifty of these wagons were made in Plymouth, Wisconsin, around the year 1900. The Pollesch brothers (Darrell, Ken, Roger, and Lynn) are avid tractor collectors with ten or twelve nicely restored Oliver, Hart-Parr, and Cletrac tractors, plus others awaiting restoration and many implements. When asked if any of the wives object to the growing collection, Lynn said, "Oh, we take new additions over to Dad's place for awhile."

was truly an awesome machine. The tractor was available with a six-cylinder gasoline engine, or a choice of a six-cylinder Oliver diesel engine

Next page
Oliver Super 66
The Super 66 was built between 1954 and 1958. It used a four-cylinder engine with increased horsepower over the plain 66. The compression ratio for the gasoline version shown here was 7.0:1. For the optional diesel, the compression ratio was 15.0:1. This adjustable wide-front variation belongs to Sam Lulich of Mason, Wisconsin. He is only the third owner since 1955. It has the live PTO, but no hydraulics.

or a blown three-cylinder, two-cycle General Motors 3–71 diesel engine. Governed speed of all versions was 1675rpm. A six-speed transmission replaced the four-speed unit of the "plain" 99.

The Oliver engines were 4.00x4.00in bore and stroke engines

Previous page
Oliver Super 99 Diesel
Setting in a field of trefoil, Charlie Lulich's big 1955 Oliver Super 99 Diesel looks better than the day it was built. Charlie, owner of Lulich Implement, Mason, Wisconsin, acquired the tractor from Meyers Salvage in Aberdeen, South Dakota. Finding the engine stuck, when he got it home, Charlie pulled the tractor and the engine broke loose. Putting in fresh fuel, Charlie pulled it again and it started! That, after being in the salvageyard for about five years.

of 302ci displacement. A compression ratio of 15.5:1 was used for the diesel and 7.0:1 for the gasoline.

The three-cylinder, 213ci General Motors engine used a bore and stroke of 4.25x5.00in and a compression ratio of 17.0:1. This engine used a Rootes-type blower to purge exhaust gasses and to supercharge the compression. No intake valves were used, but the pistons uncovered intake ports when at the bottom of their strokes. When these ports were uncovered, the conventional exhaust valves opened and the blower then swept exhaust gasses out. The

Oliver Super 99 Diesel
Oliver was among of the first tractor makers to effectively use the diesel engine. Pictured here is the six-cylinder four-cycle Oliver diesel installed in a 1955 Oliver Super 99.

General Motors designation for this engine was 3–71, or three cylinders of 71ci each (213ci, total).

Because it was a two-cycle, at 1675rpm it sounded more like it was turning 3350rpm. The blower also added to the sound so that a Super 99 in full flight howls like a ban-

shee. Also because of blower exhaust scavenging, the General Motors engine lost power quickly if the rpm decreased. Therefore, unlike other diesels, it was best to keep it howling at all times.

The Super 99 also featured an available torque converter, an optional factory cab, and the draft-control three-point hitch. Top speed in road gear for the General Motors-powered version was almost 15mph. For some reason, the advertised speed of the Oliver diesel was about 1mph slower. Originally built in the South Bend plant, production of the Super 99 was transferred to Charles City in 1958.

Oliver Super 99 GM
Built in the South Bend, Indiana, plant until the last year of production (1958), the Super 99 GM was the largest, most powerful tractor of its time. For the Nebraska Tractor Test, Number 556, the Super 99 GM weighed in at 15,055lb. More than 12,000lb were on the rear wheels!

Oliver Super 44 Utility
1957–1958

Utility tractors were pioneered by the Ford-Ferguson in 1939. The success of the type encouraged other makers to jump on the bandwagon in the mid-Fifties. Although not well-defined, the utility tractor was generally lower than row-crops and had adjustable front and rear wheel width spacing, unlike the standard-treads. The kingpins extended downward from the outer ends of the front axles, instead of from the straight axles of the standard-tread. The low, stable stance of the utility tractor made it ideal for use with the hydraulic front-end loaders, which were just becoming popular.

The Oliver Super 55, introduced in 1954, was Oliver's first true utility tractor, but the Super 44, introduced in 1957, was the first to carry the name. It originated in the Battle Creek, Michigan, plant that had built the big Nichols & Shepard machines in the Twenties.

The Super 44 Utility used a Continental four-cylinder engine of 140ci. Bore and stroke was 3.20x 4.40in. Engine operating speed was 1800rpm. This engine was of the L-head type, the first ever used by Oliver or Hart-Parr.

A four-speed transmission provided working speeds between 2–12mph. The tractor was equipped with an internal hydraulic system with which to operate the three-point hitch or remote cylinders.

An interesting feature of the Super 44 Utility was the offset (to the right) seat and steering wheel. This was ostensibly done to give the operator a better view of the field.

Oliver Super 44 Utility
George Lulich's 1957 Oliver Super 44 Utility was once a mowing tractor for a Kentucky county highway department. It used a hydraulically operated Superior mower, which has since been removed. The tractor was not tested at the University of Nebraska, but was in the 25hp class.

Oliver Super 44 Utility

Built in the factory in Battle Creek, Michigan, as the big Nichols & Shepard threshers and traction engines of the early part of the century, this little Oliver Super 44 Utility marked a significant departure from the usual Oliver tractors of the time. It was powered by a Continental engine of 140ci of the L-head design, the first ever for an Oliver or Hart-Parr tractor; the seat was off-set to right to allow the steering shaft to pass alongside the engine; and it was the lightest Oliver at 2,000lb. The 1957 example shown is owned by George Lulich of Mason, Wisconsin.

Some have speculated, however, that the designers had finished the tractor when they discovered that they'd forgotten the steering. Not letting the oversight bother them too much, they simply added it off to one side. The fact that the steering box protrudes through the grille, and the tie rod projects out the front like a bumper, lends credence to this speculation.

In 1958, production was transferred to Charles City, along with the Super 99. The Super 44 Utility, which weighed about 2,000lb, was not tested by the University of Nebraska.

The Three-Numbered Series: Oliver 550 1958–1975

The Oliver 550 was an improved replacement for the Super 55 Utility. Unlike the Super 55, the 550 could be ordered with fixed wheel tread. The 2000rpm engine could be obtained in either a gasoline or diesel version. Displacement of the four-cylinder engine was increased to 155ci, from 144ci, by increasing the bore 0.125in. The engine was equipped with aluminum pistons.

A constant-mesh, helical gear transmission was also new for the 550. It offered six speeds and a top speed of 15mph. A two-speed, live PTO was standard, as was the hydraulic three-point hitch.

Optional equipment included power-adjusted rear wheel spacing, deluxe seat, cold-weather coolant heater, swinging drawbar, and power steering.

When White took over, the 550 was restyled with a new grille. After the inclusion of Cockshutt into the White family, the tractor was sold in Canada as the Cockshutt 550.

Oliver 770 1958–1967

As with all the "three-numbered" tractors, a new paint scheme was used for the 770, which replaced the

Oliver XO-121
The experimental Oliver XO-121 tractor. The engine was a special conversion of a four-cylinder 199ci diesel block with a 12.0:1 compression-ratio head. The engine was designed for fuel efficiency with high-octane gasoline. This engine produced 57.5 corrected brake horsepower at a specific fuel consumption of 0.385lb of fuel per brake horsepower hour. The XO-121 is now housed in the Floyd County Historical Society's museum in Charles City, Iowa.

Oliver Models 660 and 550
Oliver stablemates of circa 1960, a Model 660 and a Model 550, grace the display area at the 1992 Freeport (Illinois) thresheree. *Robert N. Pripps*

Oliver Model 770

Meadow green and clover white paint were used on the new three-numbered series tractors introduced by Oliver in 1958. The 1961 Model 770 shown is owned by Charlie Lulich of Mason, Wisconsin. It was the first tractor Charlie's dad, Frank Lulich, Sr., sold after opening Lulich Implement Company, an Oliver dealership. Records show this 770 was sold for $3,800.

Super 77: meadow green with clover white wheels and trim.

The engine options were the same for the 770 as were offered for the Super 77, except the governed speed was increased to 1750rpm, from 1600rpm. The compression ratios were raised to 7.3:1 for gasoline and liquefied petroleum gas and 16.0:1 for the diesel. These changes accounted for an almost 10 percent power increase across the board.

New for the 770 (and the 880) was "Power-Booster" drive, the equivalent of International Harvester's "torque-amplifier." This was a power shift auxiliary transmission installed ahead of the master clutch that provided a 1.32:1 ratio increase when activated. This device effec-

tively gave the tractors twelve forward speeds and four in reverse. The power shift feature meant that the operator could get a half-step downshift without interrupting the power flow. This was often enough to get through the tough spot, where direct-drive could be again selected without stopping.

Another highlight of the three-numbered series, including the 770, but excluding the 550, was a new "Power-Traction" hitch. The lower links of the hitch were attached to the frame well forward on the underside of the tractor. These, plus a top link, caused draft loads to bear down on all four wheels, but mostly on the rears. Regular three-point hitch implements could be used.

The 770 was available in row-crop, Wheatland, orchard, and a variety of industrial configurations. Row-crops could be ordered in dual narrow, single front wheel, or wide (utility) front ends. The Wheatland replaced the old standard-tread machines. They were essentially row-crop tractors with straight front axles mounted under the front. After the 1962 amalgamation with White and Cockshutt, the 770 was sold in Canada in Cockshutt livery as the Cockshutt 770.

Oliver 880 1958–1963

The improved Oliver 880, which replaced the Super 88, featured more powerful engines, standard power steering, Power-Booster drive, Power-Traction hitch, and power-adjusted rear wheel spacing.

Engine power was increased over that of the Super 88 through a speed increase to 1750rpm and through compression ratio increases for the three types of engines. Also new for the 880 was a helical constant-mesh transmission, replacing the spur gear-type of the previous tractors. This meant easier shifting and much quieter operation.

After 1962, the 880 was available in Canada in Cockshutt yellow.

Oliver 950 1958–1961

One of three replacements for the Super 99, the Oliver 950 was powered by either a gasoline or diesel six-cylinder engine. Bore and stroke was 4.00x4.00in, and the operating speed was 1800rpm. Otherwise, this tractor was the same as the Super 99, though restyled. It was rated to pull a six-bottom plow.

Oliver 990 1958–1961

This Super 99 replacement was essentially the same as the Super 99 GM, except 3–71 engine's governed speed was increased to 1800rpm,

Oliver 1800
The six-plow Oliver 1800. A choice of six-cylinder gasoline, LPG, or diesel engine was offered. This is the diesel version, with cab and narrow dual front.

Cockshutt 1800 Standard Diesel
A Cockshutt 1800 Standard with diesel engine; LPG and gasoline engines were also available. This is a Series C version (1963), which boasted 72 drawbar and 84 PTO horsepower.

Oliver 1900 Standard
The Monarch of Pull. A 1960 Oliver 1900 Standard, rated to pull an eight-bottom plow. Powered by a GM 4–53 blown two-cycle, four-cylinder engine, the 1900 developed more than 100 PTO horsepower.

from 1675rpm. The 990 was rated a seven-plow tractor.

Oliver 995 Lugmatic 1958–1961

This was the same tractor as the 990, except that the GM 3–71 engine's rated speed was further upped to 2000rpm and a torque converter was installed ahead of the master clutch in the drive train. The two-cycle GM engine did not fare well when dragged down in speed, but adding the torque converter kept the speed from dropping below the most efficient speed and aided in starting heavy loads in higher gears. The torque converter doubled the pulling capacity so that the 995 was rated for twelve to fourteen plows.

Oliver 660 1959–1964

The 660 series of tractors (row-crop and high-crop), improved replacements for the Super 66 line, now received a full three-plow rating. This was made possible by increasing the bore diameter by 0.125in to 3.625in, by increasing the operating speed to 2000rpm, and by raising the compression ratio to 7.75:1 for the gasoline version. Power steering, "Powerjuster" rear wheels, the Hydra-Lectric hydraulic lift system, and three-point hitch were options.

The 660 was not tested at the University of Nebraska.

Oliver 440 1960

The 440 was a revival of the Super 44, last made at Charles City in 1958. It was essentially unchanged. No University of Nebraska tests were made on the 440.

Oliver 500 1960–1963

In a rather strange move, Oliver imported from England the Model 500, which was similar to its own 550. The 500 was a David Brown Model 850 with Oliver styling. The engine was available in either gasoline or diesel versions, and had a bore and stroke of 3.50x4.00in. The displacement of 154ci was only 1ci less than that of the 550, although power was somewhat less. Both had operating speeds of 2000rpm. A six-speed transmission was standard, as was a differential lock and the three-point hitch with draft control. Options included Powerjuster wheels, power steering, and remote hydraulic controls.

The Oliver 500 was not tested at Nebraska, but the David Brown 850 was. Its test data is included in Chapter Seven as the Oliver 500.

The Four-Numbered Series: Oliver 1800 A 1960–1962

The four-numbered tractors brought Oliver styling right up to the minute. The 1800 was a six-bottom tractor available with six-cylinder gasoline, liquefied petroleum gas, or diesel engines. The gasoline and liquefied petroleum gas versions were the same as the 265ci unit in the Oliver 880, except the rpm was raised to 2000, from 1750. The diesel was larger, at 283ci.

The 1800 was equipped with a helical-gear six-speed transmission. The PTO offered a choice of 540 or 1000rpm or direct engine speed. Either dual narrow-front wheels or adjustable wide-front was offered. Other versions were available later.

Oliver 1900 A 1960–1962

This tractor used a four-cylinder, two-cycle General Motors 4–53 engine with blower, operating at 2000rpm. It was available in Wheatland and Riceland models only. It had the same PTO system and the same live hydraulic system as the 1800. It was originally equipped with the same six-speed transmission, but later tractors had a semi-automatic Hydra-Power drive.

Cockshutt 1900
Powered by a GM 4–53 engine, the 1900 was rated for an eight-bottom plow. The drawbar horsepower rating was 90. After 1962, certain Oliver tractors were given Cockshutt nameplates for sale in Canada.

White-Oliver 1655
The White-Oliver 1655 tractor, circa 1970. A thoroughly competitive 70hp machine with three optional auxiliary transmissions: Hydra-power Drive, Over/Under Hydraul-Shift, or Creeper Drive. This one is shown at the Stephenson County Antique Engine Club's 1992 thresheree featuring Olivers. The show is held annually in Freeport, Illinois. *Robert N. Pripps*

Chapter 6

The Cockshutt Plow Company

I have walked many a weary mile behind a plow
and I know all the drudgery of it.
—*Henry Ford*

The JGC Sulky Plow made the Cockshutt Plow Company. It was invented by James G. Cockshutt in the late 1870s. Among its patented features was a unique cam arrangement for raising and lowering the plow. The vast expanse of western Canada, with its virgin sod, made the JGC Sulky Plow much in demand. As the pithy saying of Henry Ford, above, suggests, the riding plow was a real boon to farmers. The work of handling a walking plow tested the endurance of the most willing plowman. The sulky increased his working capacity and lightened his task.

James G. Cockshutt was the grandson of James and Mary Cockshutt. Mary's maiden name was Nightingale; she was the sister of Florence Nightingale, the founder of the nursing profession. The Cockshutts emigrated to Canada from Colve, Lancashire, England in 1827, bringing their two children, Ignatius and Jane.

The elder Cockshutt set up a retailing business in the village of Muddy York, now known as Toronto, but later moved it to Brantford, Ontario. Ignatius later took over the business from his father, and expected that his own son, James G., would do likewise.

James G. Cockshutt, however, was bent in another direction. He had a high degree of mechanical aptitude and an inventive turn of mind, and wanted to pursue a business of making farm tools. He perceived that agriculture was on the verge of a boom, as western lands were opened up by the railroads, and that there would be a great demand for farm equipment. His father, who was by then a leading merchant in the community, opposed the idea, considering the "blacksmith" business demeaning. James obtained financial help from other family members and started his implement business in 1877. His father would not lend any assistance in these early days.

The business was originally called the Brantford Plow Works. Its products were plows, cultivators, rollers, and planters. The plows were wood and cast iron, with steel bracing. James obtained patents on several items, including his sulky plow.

The Cockshutt Plow Company

By 1882, expansion forced incorporation; the new name was the Cockshutt Plow Company. James G. Cockshutt was president, and surprisingly, father Ignatius was vice-president. The business employed about fifty workers. Power for production was supplied by several 40hp steam engines.

Unfortunately, it was at this time that James G. Cockshutt contracted tuberculosis, probably from the intense long hours spent at the business. He moved to Redlands, California, in an effort to regain his health, but to no avail. He died in 1885 at the young age of thirty-four. Other members of the Cockshutt family closed ranks to protect the company for the sake of their investments, the employees, and for James' young family. Descendants bearing the Cockshutt name managed the company until 1957.

Cockshutt 80
This beautifully restored Cockshutt 80 is owned by Walter Kellor of Forest Junction, Wisconsin. Kellor's business is Kellor Structures, an industrial building concern. The tractor is one of many in the collection of Walter, his son Bruce, and grandson Jason.

IMPORTANT

Previous page
Cockshutt 80
Walter Kellor's Cockshutt 80 stands
before Ruben Schaefer's barn near
Forest Junction, Wisconsin. Seventy-
five year old Ruben was born on this
farm. It was farmed by his father and
grandfather before him.

By 1903, the Cockshutt Plow
Company employed 900. It had a
new plant on a 33-acre site, and a
thoroughly modern heat treatment
furnace fired by natural gas from a
well on the property. New lines
were being added regularly and now
included seeders, planters, new steel
plows, and discs.

As traction engines came on the
scene, Cockshutt scored another first
with its patented "multi-furrow," or
gang plow. Versions could plow up
to twelve 14in furrows at one time
behind one of the giant steam or
gasoline tractors. The largest of these
plows weighed 6 tons. Cockshutt
gang plows were extremely popular
in both Canada and the United
States.

The success of the gang plow
business added to the financial re-
quirements of the Cockshutt Plow
Company to the point where the
family could no longer supply the
resources. In 1910, a stock issue was
floated, and the company went public. With the new working capital,
the company expanded; twelve new
buildings and 400 new employees
were added. Adams Wagon Company, Brantford Carriage Company,
and Frost and Wood Company were
acquired.

The new subsidiaries added greatly to the Cockshutt line of products.
In addition to a full complement of
carriages and wagons, Frost and
Wood, which was founded in 1838,
was in the business of building and
selling binders, mowers, and rakes.
The acquisitions also provided the
company with nationwide branch-
office and distribution systems.

World War I found the Cockshutt
Plow Company able to help with the

war effort. Wagons and carriages
were provided to the military in
great numbers. Farm equipment was
exported in ship-load quantities to
England. At one point during these
trying times, according to an article
by W. Ashton Cockshutt, a ship containing nine carloads of farm implements, bound for England, was lost.
It was not lost to the enemy, but just
missing. After about six months, the
company received a demurrage bill
(charges for failing to unload in the
specified time) from the Port of New
Orleans.

World War I affected the Cockshutt Plow Company in another
way, as well. Seven of the Cockshutt
men served in the Armed Forces.
Sadly, Harvey Cockshutt, the only
son of the founder, was killed in
France in 1915.

After the war, the company continued to prosper until the Depression. As prices for farm commodities
dropped, the problem of selling new
farm implements and collecting
past-due accounts became insur-
mountable.

It was at this time that a remark-
able new device, called a "Tiller-
combine," was brought out by Cockshutt. It combined the tilling and
planting function into one machine
operation. The savings in fuel and
labor costs made the implement a
real necessity to the farmer in these
dire economic times. Despite how
much farmers needed this machine,
though, few had the resources with
which to acquire it. The challenge to
the salesman was not to sell the machine, but to not waste his time on
those who did not have the means to
buy it. Even in its first year, 1930,
Cockshutt salesmen were able to sell
100 Tiller-combines. In subsequent
years, as conditions improved, the
Tiller-combine did much to keep the
company prosperous.

World War II again found the
Cockshutt Company involved in the
war effort. The Brantford plant built
aircraft landing gear components
and wooden fuselages for the de

Havilland Mosquito bomber. Other
plants built ambulance bodies, gun
mounts, and 100,000 hand grenades
per month. Employment reached an
all-time high of 6,000. Toward the
end of the war, the company designed, built, and began testing a
new line of tractors and self-propelled combines.

During the post-World War II period, the Cockshutt Plow Company
continued to prosper and expand,
opening a manufacturing and marketing center in Bellevue, Ohio. Extremely hard times hit the agricultural equipment builders again in
1954, with much over-capacity as a
result of wartime expansion. Cockshutt experienced financial reversals
that caused its stock to plummet,
from more than $24 per share to less
than $8. As book value of the stock
was about $24, the company was
ripe for a takeover. This happened in
1957, when controlling interest was
acquired by the English Transconti-
nental Company.

By 1959, profitable times had returned to the firm, now known as
the Cockshutt Farm Equipment
Company of Canada, Ltd. It soon became apparent, however, that the
new owners had purchased the company for its breakup value, rather
than to continue the business. In
1961, part of the manufacturing
plant in Brantford and the rights to
the harvester/combine lines were

Next page
Cockshutt 30
The Cockshutt 30 was a three-plow
tractor with a maximum PTO
horsepower of 30.3 (Nebraska Test
Number 382). It was equipped with a
four-speed transmission, but offered an
optional under-drive to give it
effectively eight speeds forward and two
in reverse. The engine was a four-
cylinder Buda of 153ci. The tractor was
offered, during its years of production
(1946–1956), in gasoline, distillate,
diesel, and LPG versions. The Cockshutt
30 was the world's first tractor to have a
live, or independent, PTO of the type
that has since become conventional.

Cockshutt 30

The Cockshutt 30 was the first Canadian-built tractor tested at the University of Nebraska, Test Number 382 in 1947. It was also sold as the Co-Op E-3. The 30 shown is a 1950 model, owned by Jim Grant of Georgetown, Ontario. It was photographed at the Ontario Agricultural Museum.

sold to White Motor Corporation. The rest of the plant was demolished, and the manufacturing equipment sold.

Cockshutt Tractors

Before World War II, the Cockshutt Plow Company had been marketing tractors in Canada built by Oliver. These were identical to Oliv-er tractors, except the styled agricultural ones were painted a bright red with cream wheels and grille. Even before the relationship with Oliver, Cockshutt marketed Hart-Parr tractors in Canada between 1924 and 1928.

In 1928, an agreement was formed with Allis-Chalmers to market its tractors with Cockshutt nameplates. This relationship lasted for only five years. In 1934, the Hart-Parr (Oliver) line was back in Cockshutt livery.

Cockshutt 30 1946–1956

The Cockshutt 30 was the first Canadian tractor tested by the University of Nebraska beginning May 21, 1947. The 30 used a Buda four-cylinder, valve-in-head, four-cycle engine of 153ci. Bore and stroke was 3.44x4.13in. Rated speed was 1650rpm. Two versions of the engine were provided at the start: gasoline, with a compression ratio of 6.18:1; and distillate, with a compression ratio of 4.7:1. Added later were a diesel and a liquefied petroleum gas version, with ratios of 15.0:1 and 7.12:1, respectively.

The Cockshutt 30 used a four-speed transmission, but an optional under-drive unit gave eight speeds forward and two in reverse. A live PTO was featured, for which Cockshutt gets much credit for pioneering.

Work on the Cockshutt 30 began in 1944. A task force of engineers

evaluated features of several tractors and a wide variety of engines before settling on the configuration. Production of the 30 began in 1946, with just a few hundred made. The year 1947 saw production begin in earnest. The 30 was an "only-child" until 1949, when the 40 was added to the line.

The Cockshutt 30 was also sold as the Co-Op E3 and the Gamble Farmcrest 30.

Cockshutt 40 1949–1957

A six-cylinder Buda engine powered the Cockshutt 40. It was available in gasoline, distillate, and diesel versions. Compression ratios and bore and stroke were the same as for the 30 engines, but the 40 used six, rather than four, cylinders. The displacement was 230ci. Rated operating speed was 1650rpm.

A six-speed transmission was standard of the 40; no underdrive unit was offered. Like the Oliver transmission, this one had two reverse speeds. Hydraulics and a live PTO were optional.. Like the 30, the 40 was available with two front axle configurations: narrow dual and fixed wide-front. The 40 used over-

Cockshutt 40

The Cockshutt 40, like the 50, used over-the-engine steering. Tested at Nebraska in 1950, test Number 442, the 40 demonstrated a maximum pull of 5,538lb at a speed of 1.38mph.

the-engine steering. The Co-Op E4 was essentially the same as the Cockshutt 40.

Cockshutt 20 1952–1958

One of the cutest and best-performing little tractors ever made, the Cockshutt 20 is much in demand today by collectors. It was originally

Previous page
Cockshutt 40 Deluxe
This Cockshutt 40 Deluxe was built in Brantford, Ontario, Canada, in 1957. Its owner and restorer is Jim Grant of Georgetown, Ontario.

powered by a Continental F-124 engine. During the first year of production, however, the engine was changed to a Continental F-140. These engine designations stood for the displacement. Gasoline and distillate versions were offered. The stroke of all versions was 4.38in.

The bore of the smaller engine was 3.00in, and 3.20in on the larger. Compression ratios were 6.75:1 for gasoline and 5.03:1 for distillate. Operating speed was 1800rpm.

The 20 used a four-speed transmission and was offered with an optional hydraulics and live PTO. It was also sold as the Co-Op E2.

Cockshutt 50 and D-50 1953–1957

The Cockshutt 50 used Buda six-cylinder engines of 273ci displacement. These were essentially the same as the 40 engine, except cylin-

Cockshutt 40 Deluxe
This 1958 Cockshutt 40 Deluxe uses a Buda six-cylinder gasoline engine of 230ci. The Cockshutt 40 was built in Canada from 1949–1957. The 40's engine was available in gasoline, distillate, and diesel versions. It was essentially the same engine as used in the Cockshutt 30, except with six, rather than four, cylinders.

der sleeves were not used, giving the engine a bore of 3.75in. The compression ratio was increased for the gasoline version to 6.6:1, and re-

Cockshutt 20

The Cockshutt 20 was sold in gasoline and distillate versions. The Continental engines boasted fairly high compression ratios, for the time (1952–1958); 6.75:1 for the gasoline and 5.03:1 for the distillate. The gasoline version (shown) was the more popular. Its 140ci displacement and 1800rpm operating speed gave it a maximum power rating of 28hp. This and its 4,500lb weight made it the power equal of the John Deere Model B.

Cockshutt 20

Initially powered by a Continental F-124 engine, the Cockshutt 20 was soon revised to use the Continental F-140 engine for more power. The engine designations indicate displacement in cubic inches. Shown is Jim Grant's 1954 Cockshutt 20, photographed at The Great Canadian Antique Tractor Field Days, on the grounds of the Ontario Agricultural Museum.

duced for the diesel to 14.3:1. No distillate engine was offered. Rated rpm remained at 1650. Hydraulics and a live PTO were optional.

The 50 was actually the same tractor as the 40, but with increased engine displacement and larger tires. The Model 50 was also sold as the Co-Op E5.

Cockshutt 40D4 and Golden Eagle 1954–1957

After Cockshutt bought out the National Farm Equipment Co-Op, in Bellevue, Ohio, the Model 40 tractor was marketed in the United States as the Golden Eagle and in Canada as the 40D4. Both versions were avail-able only with four-cylinder Perkins diesels, as Allis-Chalmers had acquired Buda by then. The only other difference between Golden Eagle and the 40 was a special red and yellow paint job.

Cockshutt 35 and Blackhawk 35 1956–1957

These tractors replaced the 30 in Canada and the United States after the Buda engine was replaced by a Hercules of 198ci.

Cockshutt 500 Series 1958–1962

In 1957, Cockshutt engaged the services of noted industrial designer, Raymond Lowey, who had attained recent fame for his radical 1953

Cockshutt 20 Deluxe
Jim Grant's 1958 Cockshutt 20 Deluxe, serial number 40069, shown on the grounds of the Ontario Agricultural Museum. Jim resides in Georgetown, Ontario.

Studebaker car designs. The styling and design of the Lowey Cockshutt tractor was strikingly purposeful and beautiful. Four series were included: the 540 gas, 550 gas or diesel, 560 diesel, and 570 gas or diesel.

The displacement of the 550's Hercules four-cylinder engine was 198ci; for the 560, a four-cylinder

Cockshutt D-50
The Cockshutt D-50 was truly an impressive tractor. Using a six-cylinder Buda diesel engine, the tractor produced a maximum PTO horsepower of 53 and 47hp on the drawbar. For its time (1953–1957), these power ratings put it in the big leagues. Jim Grant of Georgetown, Ontario, is the owner of this 1954 model. It was photographed at the Great Canadian Tractor Farm Field Days in Milton, Ontario.

Perkins of 269.5ci; and for the 570, a six-cylinder 298ci Hercules. All engines operated at 1650rpm, used the six-speed transmission, and offered live PTO and hydraulics.

Cockshutt 35
The Cockshutt 35 was essentially the same as the Cockshutt 40, but replaced the Cockshutt 30 in the lineup after the engine change to the Hercules 198ci unit.

Cockshutt 35 Deluxe
This Cockshutt 35 Deluxe was built in Canada in 1956. The Cockshutt 35 was not tested at the University of Nebraska, but was rated by Cockshutt at 33 drawbar horsepower. This 35 is owned by Jim Grant of Georgetown, Ontario. It is shown at the Ontario Agricultural Museum in Milton, Ontario.

Cockshutt 550
The Cockshutt 550 was available in either gas or diesel form from 1958 through 1962.

Chapter 7

Nebraska Test Data

The last of the great [tractor] demonstrations was held
[in Fargo, North Dakota, in 1917]. A tragic outcome
of this meeting was the death of five horses entered in
competition with the tractors—martyrs to a lost cause.
—*Arch Merritt*

Early power farmers were more often than not the victims of over-sold, under-designed tractors. First, dissemination of information in those days was nothing like we enjoy today. Unless someone in your neighborhood had a particular type of tractor, you were not likely to hear much about it. This was also true of other pieces of machinery and automobiles. Second, being rural meant being isolated. Newspapers came by mail several days after the publishing date; radio was in its infancy; publication of farming journals was just beginning. And finally, there were no standards by which mechanical things could be measured.

Because there were so many of them in those days, farmers had particular clout with the state legislatures. They began to clamor for a na-

Oliver Super 99
First built in Oliver's South Bend plant, production of the Super 99 was later transferred to Charles City. This 1955 example is owned by Dick Ramminger of Morrisonville, Wisconsin.

tional rating system for tractors, so that at least the power capability of a tractor could be understood. Competitive tractor trials in Winnipeg and other Canadian and US cities pointed out disparities between advertising claims and actual performance. These tractors in these trials were often heavily modified by the factory, and an army of mechanics and engineers kept them running long enough to compete. National legislation became bogged down in politics, however, and never came to pass.

A Nebraska farmer, named Wilmot F. Crozier, who had also been a school teacher (to support the farm, he said), purchased a "Ford" tractor from the Minneapolis outfit not related to Henry Ford. The tractor was so unsatisfactory that he demanded the company replace it. The replacement was worse. He then bought a Bull tractor. This, too, was completely unsatisfactory. Next, he bought a 1918 Rumely "three-plow." The Rumely met, and exceeded, Crozier's expectations. Not only did it stand up to the strains of farming, he was able to regularly pull a five-bottom plow. Shortly afterward,

Crozier was elected to the Nebraska legislature.

In 1919, Representative Crozier and Senator Charles Warner introduced legislation that resulted in the "Nebraska Test Law." This law required that any tractor sold in Nebraska had to be certified by the state. The state was to test the tractors to ensure that they lived up to their advertised claims. The tests were to be conducted by the University of Nebraska, Agricultural Engineering Department. L. W. Chase and Claude Shedd devised the tests and the test equipment, which have become standards for the world.

The first test was made in the fall of 1919 (things happened a lot faster in those days) of a Twin City 12–20, but could not be completed because of snowfall. The first complete test was made in the spring of 1920. A certificate was issued for the Waterloo Boy Model N.

Notes on Nebraska Tractor Tests

Fuel: K=Kerosene; Dis.=Distillate; D=Diesel; LPG=Liquefied petroleum gas, or propane.

Belt/PTO Horsepower: This is Test C horsepower, the maximum attainable at the PTO or belt pulley. If the generator, hydraulic pump, etc., were not standard equipment, they were removed for these tests. Note that Nebraska test data published during this period are not corrected to standard atmospheric conditions.

Drawbar Horsepower: Taken from Test G data, it is based on maximum drawbar pull and speed. The difference between this and PTO horsepower is due to slippage, and to the power required to move the tractor itself. The heavier the tractor, the less the slippage, but the more power required to move the tractor. Factory engineers looked for the ideal compromise.

Maximum Pull: Test G. The pull used for calculating drawbar horsepower.

Fuel Consumption: The rate of fuel consumption in horsepower hours per gallon taken from Test C conditions. The higher the number, the better.

Pull: Measured in pounds.

Weight: The weight of the tractor plus ballast in pounds. Ballast was often added for Test G and other heavy pulling tests, and then removed for other tests to improve performance.

Wheels: Steel or rubber.

Oliver Nebraska Tractor Tests Summary

Model	Test Number	Fuel	Max. HP Belt/PTO	Max. HP Drawbar	Max. Pull	Fuel use	Weight	Wheels	Year
Oliver Hart-Parr Tractors									
18–27	176	K	29.7	NA	3664	9.7	4650	S	1930
18–28	180	K	30.3	23.6	3241	10	4420	S	1930
28–44	183	K	49.0	28.4	5116	10	6415	S	1930
Oliver Tractors									
70	252	G	26.6	18.0	3120	11.1	3500	S	1936
80	365	G	38.1	32.7	5079	11.5	8145	R	1940
99	451	G	59.0	46.4	7594	11.5	10193	R	1950
60	375	G	18.4	15.2	2496	12.2	3245	R	1941
88	388	G	42.0	37.0	5173	11.6	5285	R	1947
88	450	D	43.5	38.3	5869	12.9	7639	R	1950
77	404	G	34.0	28.7	4079	11.5	4828	R	1948
77	457	D	35.8	27.8	4818	14.5	7210	R	1951
66	412	G	23.9	NA	3207	12.0	5561	R	1949
66	467	D	25.0	22.1	3571	14.2	5717	R	1951
Super 55	524	G	34.4	29.6	3539	11.4	5501	R	1954
Super 66	544	D	33.7	28.0	4393	14.2	6726	R	1955
Super 77	543	D	44.1	38.1	5659	14.8	8600	R	1955
Super 88	527	D	58.1	50.0	6287	15.2	9446	R	1954
Super 99	556	GMD	78.7	73.3	10000+	13.3	15055	R	1955
Super 99	557	O-D	62.4	50.4	9212	14.1	13311	R	1955
550	697	G	41.4	35.5	5149	12.5	6815	R	1959
770	649	D	48.8	44.4	7137	14.3	8755	R	1958
880	650	D	59.5	52.6	8118	14.8	10165	R	1958
990	661	GMD	84.1	70.1	12K+	13.4	16230	R	1958
995	662	GMD	85.4	71.4	12K+	12.6	16305	R	1958
500	734	D	33.6	31.8	2536	15.5	5874	R	1960
1800	766	G	73.9	61.7	4427	13.2	14335	R	1960
1800	767	D	70.2	62.6	4472	14.2	14345	R	1960
1900	768	D	89.4	82.9	6282	14.4	16665	R	1960
Cockshutt Tractors									
20	474	G	28.9	25.5	3266	10.7	4491	R	1952
30	382	G	30.3	23.6	3743	11.4	NA	R	1947
40	442	G	43.3	37.9	5538	11.3	8371	R	1950
50	487	D	53.3	47.2	6319	14.6	10655	R	1952
50	488	G	57.8	51.5	6463	12.2	NA	R	1952

Model	Test Number	Fuel	Max. HP Belt/PTO	Max. HP Drawbar	Max. Pull	Fuel use	Weight	Wheels	Year
550	681	D	38.5	34.5	6544	15.5	7735	R	1958
560	682	D	48.5	45.6	NA	17.7	9445	R	1958
570	683	D	60.8	52.3	9063	15.0	11355	R	1958
Competitors' Tractors									
Fordson	124	K	22.3	12.3	2142	8.95	3175	S	1926
Deere GP	153	K	25.0	17.2	2489	9.18	4265	S	1928
Deere A	335	Dis.	28.9	24.6	4110	11.3	6410	R	1939
Ford 8N	443	G	25.5	20.8	2810	11.2	4043	R	1950
A-C WD45	563	D	43.3	32.5	5908	14.0	9700	R	1955
Super MD	477	D	46.7	37.7	5772	13.9	9338	R	1952
Farmall.A	329	G	16.8	12.3	2387	12.0	3570	R	1939
Farmall.H	334	Dis.	22.1	19.4	3169	11.8	5550	R	1939

Epilogue

Anchored in the past for a solid future.
—*White Marketing Video*

The heritage of the Oliver and Cockshutt lines of tractors and other equipment go deep into the soil of history like the roots of an ancient oak. Just as the old oak tree weathered many a storm, so have these great concerns. Their repertoire of experience and service now resides under the name of AGCO and its White Tractor Division.

As described previously in the pages of this book, these roots go as far back as 1839, when the Canadian Frost and Wood Company was founded. This was a time of rebellion in Canada, when radicals wanted independence from England. The uprisings caused many border problems between the United States and Canada. It was the time when "Tippecanoe and Tyler Too" Tyler was President of the United States and Daniel Webster was Secretary of State. Frost and Wood later was folded into Cockshutt, which itself was founded in 1877.

The Superior Drill Company was started in 1840. Nichols & Shepard originated in 1848. The Oliver Chilled Plow Company was founded in 1855. That was six years before Abraham Lincoln was inaugurated.

Hart-Parr Gasoline Engine Company began in 1897, the year of the first American comic strip, The Katzenjammer Kids. These all became the Oliver Farm Equipment Corporation in 1929.

A parallel root comes from the Moline Plow Company, founded in 1870. Their innovative "Universal" tractor, brought out in 1917, was the first tractor capable of doing all the work of the horse; it was the first tractor with a starter, lights, and battery, and it was also the first articulated tractor. In 1929, Moline Plow joined with the Minneapolis Threshing Machine Company and Minneapolis Steel and Machinery to form the Minneapolis-Moline Power Implement Company. Avery Plow, which hailed from all the way back to 1825, was added to Minneapolis-Moline in 1951.

On November 1, 1960, just before John F. Kennedy was elected President, the White Motor Corporation of Cleveland, Ohio, a leading builder of heavy-duty trucks, bought the Oliver Corporation as a wholly owned subsidiary. In 1962, Cockshutt was added as a subsidiary to Oliver, and Minneapolis-Moline was

added in 1963. For the next several years, all continued operating under their own names, but with considerable cross-pollination of technology. In 1969, they were brought together under one banner, and the White Farm Equipment Company was born. All the technological tractor assets were combined into a new line of tractors called the White Field Boss.

The late-Seventies brought another round of economic hardships to the agricultural equipment industry, and White Farm Equipment Company found itself in need of a new financial partner. In December of 1980, the Texas Investment Corporation purchased the White Farm

Oliver 550 Utility

Sam Lulich, Jr., of Mason, Wisconsin, owns this 1966 Oliver 550 Utility tractor. It's an improved version of the original Super 55, which Oliver brought out to counter the highly successful Ford 8N. This 550 is a gasoline version; a diesel was also available. Both engines were four-cylinder units with 3.625x3.75in bore and stroke. Governed operating speed was 2000rpm. The 550 was about a 40hp tractor.

Oliver 2255
A 1973 Oliver 2255 powered by a 145hp Caterpillar V-8 of 573ci displacement. In Canada, this tractor was marketed as the White 2255. *Robert N. Pripps*

Equipment Company in its entirety as a wholly owned subsidiary.

Unfortunately, Texas Investment Corporation was just the first of several management changes to come.

Selected assets of White were purchased by Allied Products Corporation from Texas Investment in 1985. The next year, White was able to buy selected assets of its former relative north of the border, White Farm Manufacturing Company, Ltd. In May 1987, Allied merged White with another of its subsidiaries, New Idea Farm Equipment Corporation, to form White-New Idea Farm Equipment Company. Headquarters and manufacturing were in Coldwater, Ohio. In June 1991, the Allis-Gleaner Company purchased White-New Idea as a subsidiary of its Deutz-Allis Company. White was now part of the largest dealer network in North America.

In 1992, AGCO was formed as a holding company in a management buyout of White and other assets from the German owners. The offices of AGCO are in Norcross, Georgia. Soon after the buyout, production facilities were moved to Independence, Missouri, where manufacturing, quality control, and parts distribution have been modernized to be second to none.

In addition to the White Tractor Division, AGCO consists of Deutz-Allis, Heston, the Parts Division, and AGCO Farm Finance Corporation. Since being under the AGCO banner, White has introduced a line of ten new tractors. AGCO offers outstanding warranties and financing.

In the heritage of White Tractors are many firsts, including:
- First tractor plant
- First real production tractor
- First tractor advertising
- First valve-in-head tractor engine
- First live PTO
- First disk brakes
- First liquefied petroleum gas tractor engine
- First cultivating tractor
- First tractor with starter and lights
- First articulated tractor
- First kerosene-burning tractor
- First multi-speed tractor transmission
- First four-valve-per-cylinder tractor engine
- First tractor cab with radio

AGCO is dedicated to the full use of its assets and heritage to better serve North American farmers. My best to them, and to the farmers that have worked so hard through good times, and through economic storms, to feed the world.

Postscript

November 1993 marked the end of the era for the place that calls itself the birthplace of the tractor industry: Charles City, Iowa.

The White-New Idea farm equipment factory, the one opened in 1900 by Charles Hart and Charles Parr, closed for good. Its manufacturing equipment was auctioned.

From this factory, in 1901, rolled the world's first successful production tractor: Hart-Parr Number 1. In its heyday, the plant employed 3,000 workers. Thousands of Hart-Parr, Oliver, Cockshutt, and White tractors were built there over the years. About 420 people were still employed when production ceased in July.

Serial Number and Model Year-Data

The following charts provide a means of determining a tractor's model year by giving the beginning serial number for each production year.

Oliver Hart-Parr 18–27
1930	100001
1931	102649
1932	103319
1933	103618
1934	104039
1935	104851
1936	107312
1937	108574

Oliver Hart-Parr 18–28
1930	800001
1931	800460
1932	800964
1933	800985
1934	801051
1935	801241
1936	801990
1937	802938

Oliver 60 Row Crop
1940	600001
1941	600071
1942	606304
1943	607395
1944	608526
1945	612047
1946	615628
1947	616707
1948	620257

Oliver 60 Standard
1942	410001
1943	410501
1944	410511
1945	410617
1946	410911
1947	411311
1948	411961

Oliver 70 Row Crop
1935	200001
1936	200686
1937	208729
1938	219645
1939	223255
1940	231116
1941	236356
1942	241391
1943	243640
1944	244711
1945	250180
1946	252780
1947	258140
1948	262840

Oliver 70 Standard
1936	300001
1937	300634
1938	302084
1939	303465
1940	305362
1941	306594
1942	307580
1943	308188
1944	308484
1945	310218
1946	311116
1947	312699
1948	314221

Oliver 80 Row Crop
1937	109152
1938	109162
1939	109783
1940	110221
1941	110615
1942	110945
1943	111219
1944	111391
1945	111929
1946	112879
1947	114144
1948	114944

Oliver 80 Standard
1937	803929
1938	803991
1939	805377
1940	806880
1941	808880
1942	809051
1943	809991
1944	810470
1945	811991
1946	813067
1947	814564
1948	815216

Oliver 90 and 99
1937	508819
1938	508935
1940	510068
1941	510564
1942	510977
1943	511296
1944	511474
1945	512044
1946	512821
1947	513106
1948	513856
1949	514856
1950	516276
1951	516888
1952	517874
1953	518300
1954	519245
1955	519516
1956	520354
1957	520868

Oliver 66 Row Crop
1949	420001
1950	421589
1951	426001
1952	429771

Oliver 66 Standard
1949	470001
1950	470406
1951	472391
1952	474233

Oliver 77 Row Crop
1948 320001
1949 320241
1950 327901
1951 337343
1952 347904

Oliver 77 Standard
1948 269001
1949 269697
1950 271267
1951 272466
1952 273376

Oliver 88 Row Crop
1947 120001
1948 120353
1949 123301
1950 128653
1951 132863
1952 138184

Oliver 88 Standard
1947 820001
1948 820136
1949 821086
1950 824241
1951 825811
1952 826917

Oliver 66 (All Versions)
1953 3503990
1954 4500309

Oliver 77 (All Versions)
1953 3500001
1954 4501667

Oliver 88 (All Versions)
1953 3500977
1954 4500076

Oliver Super 44
1957 1002
1958 1551

Oliver Super 55
1954 6001
1955 11887
1956 35001
1957 43916
1958 56501

Oliver Super 66
1954 7085

1955 14099
1956 39371
1957 45846
1958 57858

Oliver Super 77
1954 8303
1955 10001
1956 38500
1957 44167
1958 56917

Oliver Super 88
1954 6503
1955 10075
1956 36774
1957 43901
1958 56580

Oliver Super 99
1957 521300
1958 521496

Oliver Model 440
1960 87725

Oliver Model 500
1960 100001
1961 100501
1962 101201

Oliver Model 550
1958 60501
1959 72632
1960 84416
1961 111868
1962 117541

Oliver Model 600
1962 449800

Oliver Model 660
1959 73132
1960 84554
1961 111213
1962 117873

Oliver Model 770
1958 60504
1959 71001
1960 ....NA
1961 111472
1962 117600

Oliver Model 880
1958 60505
1959 71640
1960 ....NA
1961 111262
1962 117640

Oliver Models 950, 990, and 995
1958 530001
1959 71245
1960 84487
1961 110064

Oliver Model 1800
1960 90525
1961 111025
1962 18344

Oliver Model 1900
1960 90932
1961 111028
1962 118356

Cockshutt Model 20
1952 101
1953 1657
1954 2568
1955 10001
1956 20001
1957 30001
1958 40001

Cockshutt Model 30
1946 1
1947 442
1948 6705
1949 17370
1950 26161
1951 28505
1952 32389
1953 35580
1954 35974
1955 40001
1956 50001

Cockshutt Model 35
1956 1001
1957 10001

Cockshutt Model 40
1949 101
1950 194

1951 4098
1952 6886
1953 10472
1954 11363
1955 20000
1956 30001
1957 40001

Cockshutt Model 50
1953 101
1954 1750
1955 10001
1956 20001
1957 30001

Cockshutt Model 540
1958 ....AM1001
1959 ....AN5001
1960 ....None
1961 ....AP1001
1962 ....AR1001

Cockshutt Model 550
1958 ....BM1001
1959 ....BN5001
1960 ....BO1001
1961 ....BP1001

Cockshutt Model 560
1958 ....CM1001
1959 ....CN5001
1960 ....CO7001
1961 ....CP1001

Cockshutt Model 570
1958 ....DM1001
1959 ....DN5001
1960 ....DO7001

Cockshutt Model 570 Super
1961 ....DP1001
1962 ....DR1001

Cockshutt Model 40D4 and Golden Eagle
1954 27001
1955 30001
1956 40028
1957 50001

Cockshutt Golden Arrow
1956 16001

Recommended Reading

The following books offered essential background on the origins and history of Oliver and Cockshutt, and about the tractors and equipment of the times. Most are available from Motorbooks International Publishers & Wholesalers, P.O. Box 2, 729 Prospect Avenue, Osceola, Wisconsin 54020 USA.

Gray, R.B. *The Agricultural Tractor 1855–1950*. St. Joseph, Michigan: Society of Agricultural Engineers.

Leffingwell, Randy. *The American Farm Tractor*. Osceola, Wisconsin: Motorbooks International.

White Farm Equipment Company. *A Rich Heritage, A Solid Future. Progress in Tractor Power from 1898*.

McCormick, Cyrus. *The Century of the Reaper*. Houghton Mifflin Company.

Morland, Andrew, and Nick Baldwin. *Classic American Farm Tractors*. Osprey.

King, Alan. *Data Book No.4, Oliver Hart-Parr, 1898–1975*. A collection of Oliver ads and articles by the son of Bert C. King, former director of advertising for Oliver Farm Equipment Company.

Stephens, Randy. *Farm Tractors 1926–1956*. A compilation of pages from "The Cooperative Tractor Catalog" and the "Red Tractor Book." Intertec Publishing.

Williams, Robert C. *Fordson, Farmall and Poppin' Johnny*. University of Illinois Press.

Pripps, Robert N., and Andrew Morland. *Ford Tractors*. Osceola, Wisconsin: Motorbooks International.

Williams, Michael. *Ford and Fordson Tractors*. Blandford Press.

Williams, Michael, and Andrew Morland. *Great Tractors*. Blandford Press.

Wik, Reynold M. *Henry Ford and Grassroots America*. The University of Michigan Press.

Denison, Merrill. *Harvest Triumphant*. Wm. Collins Sons & Company Ltd.

Pripps, Robert N. *How to Restore Your Farm Tractor*. Osceola, Wisconsin: Motorbooks International.

Wendell, C.H., and Andrew Morland. *Minneapolis-Moline Tractors 1870–1969*. Osceola, Wisconsin: Motorbooks International.

Wendell, C.H. *Nebraska Tractor Tests Since 1920*. Crestline Publishing.

The Oliver Book, a 1940 edition of Oliver's equipment catalog.

Hubbard, Elbert. *James Oliver; Little Journeys to the Homes of Great Business Men*. Roycrofters, 1909.

Pripps, Robert N., and Andrew Morland. *Threshers*. Osceola, Wisconsin: Motorbooks International.

The Yearbook of Agriculture—1960, US Department of Agriculture.

Morland, Andrew. *Traction Engines*. Osprey.

Wendel, C.H. *150 Years of International Harvester*. Crestline Publishing.

Other Interesting Publications

Stemgas Publishing Company issues an annual directory of Engine and Threshing Shows, available for $5. That address is P.O. Box 328, Lancaster, Pennsylvania 17603. Stemgas also publishes *Gas Engine Magazine* and *Iron-men Album*, magazines for the enthusiast.

Clubs and Newsletters

Newsletters providing a wealth of information and lore about individual brands of antique farm tractors and equipment have been on the scene for some time. More are springing up each year, so the following list is far from complete.

Antique Power
Patrick Ertel
P.O. Box 838
Yellow Springs, OH 45387

Green Magazine
(John Deere)
R. & C. Hain
R.R. 1
Bee, NE 68314

M-M Corresponder
(Minneapolis-Moline)
Roger Mohr
Rt. 1, Box 153
Vail, IA 51465

9N-2N-8N Newsletter
(Ford)
G.W. Rinaldi

154 Blackwood Ln.
Stamford, CT 06903

Old Abe's News
(Case)
David T. Erb
Rt. 2, Box 2427,
Vinton, OH 45686

Old Allis News
(Allis-Chalmers)
Nan Jones
10925 Love Rd.
Belleview, MI 49021

Oliver Collector's News
Dennis Gerszewski
Rt. 1
Manvel, ND 58256-0044

Prairie Gold Rush
(Minneapolis-Moline)

R. Baumgartner
Rt. 1
Walnut, IL 61376

Red Power
(International Harvester)
Daryl Miller
Box 277
Battle Creek, IA 51006

Two-Cylinder Clubs Worldwide
(John Deere)
Jack Cherry
P.O. Box 219
Grundy Center, IA 50638

Wild Harvest
(Massey)
Keith Oltrogge
1010 S. Powell,
Box 529
Denver, IA 50622

Index